Learning Unix for Mac OS X

Related Mac OS X Titles from O'Reilly

Essentials

AppleScript in a Nutshell
Building Cocoa Applications:
  A Step-by-Step Guide
Learning Carbon
Learning Cocoa
Mac OS X Pocket Reference
REALbasic: The Definitive Guide

Missing Manuals

AppleWorks 6: The Missing
  Manual
iMovie 2: The Missing Manual
Mac OS 9: The Missing Manual
Mac OS X: The Missing Manual
Office 2001 for Macintosh:
  The Missing Manual
Office X for Macintosh:
  The Missing Manual

Unix Essentials

Using csh & tcsh
Unix in a Nutshell
Unix Power Tools
Learning GNU Emacs
Learning the vi Editor

Related Programming

Developing Java Beans™
Java™ Cookbook
Java™ I/O
Java™ Network Programming
Java™ in a Nutshell
Learning Java™
Learning Perl
Perl in a Nutshell
Practical C Programming
Programming with Qt

Mac OS X Administration

Apache: The Definitive Guide
Essential System Administration
sendmail

Learning Unix for Mac OS X

Dave Taylor and Jerry Peek

with Grace Todino and John Strang

O'REILLY®

Beijing · Cambridge · Farnham · Köln · Paris · Sebastopol · Taipei · Tokyo

Learning Unix for Mac OS X
by Dave Taylor and Jerry Peek

Copyright © 2002 O'Reilly & Associates, Inc. All rights reserved.
Printed in the United States of America.

Published by O'Reilly & Associates, Inc., 1005 Gravenstein Highway North,
Sebastopol, CA 95472.

O'Reilly & Associates books may be purchased for educational, business, or sales pro-
motional use. Online editions are also available for most titles (*safari.oreilly.com*). For
more information, contact our corporate/institutional sales department: (800) 998-9938
or *corporate@oreilly.com*.

Editor:	Laurie Petrycki
Production Editor:	Linley Dolby
Cover Designer:	Emma Colby
Interior Designer:	David Futato

Printing History:

May 2002:	First Edition.

ISBN: 0-596-00342-0
[M]   [9/02]

Table of Contents

Preface

Mac OS X (pronounced "Mac OS Ten"), the latest incarnation of the Macintosh operating system, is a radical departure from previous versions. Not only is there a whole new look and feel (dubbed "Aqua"), there are huge differences under the hood. All the old, familiar Macintosh system software has been replaced with another operating system, called Unix. Unix is a multiuser, multitasking operating system. Being multiuser means Mac OS X allows multiple users to share the same system, each having the ability to customize the desktop, create files that can be kept private from other users, and to make settings that will automatically be restored whenever that person uses the computer. Being multitasking means the computer can easily run many different applications at the same time, and that if one application crashes or hangs, the entire system doesn't need to be rebooted.

The fact that Mac OS X is Unix under the hood doesn't matter to users who simply want to use its slick graphical interface to run their applications or manage their files. But it opens up worlds of possibilities for users who want to dig a little deeper. The Unix command-line interface, which is accessible through a Mac application called the Terminal, provides an enormous amount of power for advanced users. What's more, once you've learned to use Unix in OS X, you'll also be able to use the command line in other versions of Unix such as Linux.

This book is designed to teach the basics of Unix to Macintosh users. We tell you how to use the command line (which Unix users refer to as "the shell") and the filesystem, as well as some of the most useful commands. Unix is a complex and powerful system, so we only scratch the surface, but we also tell you how to deepen your Unix knowledge once you're ready for more.

Mac OS X and the Unix Family of Operating Systems

The Macintosh started out with a single-tasking operating system that allowed simple switching between applications through an application called the Finder. More recent versions of Mac OS have supported multiple applications running simultaneously, but it wasn't until the landmark release of Mac OS X that true multitasking arrived in the Macintosh world. With OS X, Macintosh applications run in separate memory areas. A true multiuser system that includes proper file-level security is also finally part of the Mac.

To accomplish these improvements, Mac OS X made the jump from a proprietary underlying operating environment to Unix. Mac OS X is built on top of Darwin, a version of Unix based on BSD 4.4, FreeBSD, and the Mach microkernel.

Unix itself was invented more than 30 years ago for scientific and professional users who wanted a very powerful and flexible OS. It has evolved since then through a remarkably circuitous path, with stops at Bell Telephone Labs, UC Berkeley, research centers in Australia and Europe, and the U.S. Department of Defense Advanced Research Projects Agency (for funding). Because Unix was designed for experts, it can be a bit overwhelming at first. But after you get the basics (from this book!) you'll start to appreciate some of the reasons to use Unix:

- It comes with a huge number of powerful application programs. You can get many others for free on the Internet. (The GNU utilities, available from the Free Software Foundation (*http://www.fsf.org/*), are very popular.) You can thus do much more at a much lower cost.

- Not only are the applications often free, but some Unix versions are also free. Linux is a good example. Like the free applications, most free Unix versions are of excellent quality. They're maintained by volunteer programmers who want a powerful OS and are frustrated by the slow, bug-ridden OS development at some big software companies. With Mac OS X, Unix is also "free" as part of the operating system, and many people use Mac OS X daily without ever knowing about all the power lurking under the hood.

- Unix runs on almost any kind of computer, from tiny embedded systems to giant supercomputers. After you read this book, you'll not only know all about Darwin, but you'll also be ready to use many other kinds of Unix-based computers without learning a new OS for each one.

- In general, Unix (especially without a windowing system) is less resource intensive than other major operating systems. For instance, Linux will run happily on an old system with a x386 microprocessor and let multiple users share the same computer. (Don't bother trying to use the latest versions of Microsoft Windows on a system that's more than a few years old!) If you need a windowing system, Unix lets you choose from modern feature-rich interfaces as well as from simple ones that need much less system power. Anyone with limited resources—educational institutions, organizations in developing countries, and so on—can use Unix to do more with less.

- Much of the Internet's development was done on Unix systems. Many Internet web sites and Internet service providers use Unix because it's so flexible and inexpensive. With powerful hardware, Unix really shines.

Versions of Unix

There are several versions of Unix. Some past and present commercial versions include Solaris, AIX, and HP/UX. Freely available versions include Linux, NetBSD, and FreeBSD. Darwin, the Unix underneath Mac OS X, was built by grafting an advanced version called Mach onto FreeBSD, with a light sprinkling of Apple magic for the windowing system.

Although graphical user interfaces (GUIs) and advanced features differ among Unix systems, you should be able to use much of what you learn from this introductory handbook on any system. Don't worry too much about what's from what version of Unix. Just as English borrows words from French, German, Japanese, Italian, and even Hebrew, Mac OS X Unix borrows commands from many different versions of Unix, but you can just use them all without paying attention to their origins.

We do from time to time explain features of Unix on other systems. Knowing the differences can help you if you ever want to use another type of Unix system. When we write "Unix" in this book, we mean "Unix and its versions" unless we specifically mention a particular version.

Interfaces to Unix

Unix can be used as it was originally designed: on typewriter-like terminals, from a prompt on a command line. Most versions of Unix also work with window systems (or GUIs). These allow each user to have a single screen with multiple windows—including "terminal" windows that act like the original Unix interface.

Mac OS X includes a simple terminal application for accessing the command-line level of the system. That application, reasonably enough, is called Terminal and can be found in the Applications → Utilities folder. The Terminal application will be examined more closely in Chapters 1 and 2.

Although you can certainly use your Mac quite efficiently without typing text at a shell prompt, we'll spend all our time in this book on that traditional command-line interface to Unix. Why?

- Every Unix system has a command-line interface. If you know how to use the command line, you'll always be able to use the system.

- If you become a more advanced Unix user, you'll find that the command line is actually much more flexible than a windowing interface. Unix programs are designed to be used together from the command line—as "building blocks"—in an almost infinite number of combinations, to do an infinite number of tasks. No windowing system we've seen (yet!) has this tremendous power.

- You can launch and close windowing programs from the command line, but windowing programs don't generally affect those programs.

- Once you learn to use the command line, you can use those same techniques to write *scripts*. These little (or big!) programs automate jobs you'd have to do manually and repetitively with a window system (unless you understand how to program a window system, which is usually a much harder job). See the section "Programming" in Chapter 10 for a brief introduction to scripting.

- In general, text-based interfaces are much easier than GUIs for sight-impaired users.

We aren't saying that the command-line interface is right for every situation. For instance, using the Web—with its graphics and links—is usually easier with a GUI web browser within Mac OS X. But the command line is the fundamental way to use Unix. Understanding it will let you work on any Unix system, with or without windows. A great resource for general OS X information (the GUI you're probably used to) can be found in *Mac OS X: The Missing Manual* by David Pogue (Pogue Press/O'Reilly).

What This Handbook Covers

This book teaches basic system utility commands to get you started with Unix, specifically Darwin. Instead of overwhelming you with lots of details, we want you to be comfortable in the Unix environment as soon as possible. So we cover a command's most useful features instead of describing all its options in detail.

We also assume that your computer works properly; you have started it, knows the procedure for turning the power off, and knows how to perform system maintenance. In other words, we don't cover Unix system administration or Mac system administration from the command line.

Without making substantial changes to Mac OS X, Darwin users are constrained to using Aqua (the standard Mac system) as the graphical interface to the system. On a non-Mac Unix system, users can choose between many different user interfaces—shells and window systems. If you do advanced work or set up Unix systems for other users, we recommend learning about a variety of shells and window systems and choosing the best ones for your needs. The principles explained in this book should help you use any Unix configuration.

Format

The following sections describe conventions used in this handbook.

Graphical User Interface Features

While this book spends most of its time on the Unix command line, we do sometimes need to tell you how to run programs from the GUI. We may do this with a compact syntax such as:

Finder → Applications → Utilities → Terminal

This shorthand should be read as: open the Finder, then choose Applications, then Utilities, then Terminal. We use the same syntax whether the user interface feature to be selected is a window, a menu item, or an icon. The meaning should be obvious from the context. If you don't see a window or icon with the name we give, look at the menu bar. (For example, Terminal → Preferences means to select the Preferences item from the Terminal's menu bar.)

Unix Commands

We introduce each main concept first, then break it down into task-oriented sections. Each section shows the best command to use for a task, explains what it does, and shows the syntax (how to put the command line together). The syntax is given like this:

    rm *filename*

Commands appear in constant width type (in this example, rm). You should type the command exactly as it appears in the example. The variable parts (here, *filename*) will appear in *constant width italic* type; you must supply your own value. To enter this command, you would type rm followed by a space and the name of the file that you want to remove, then press the Return key. (Your keyboard may have a key labeled Enter or an arrow with a right-angle shaft instead of a Return key.) Throughout this book, the term *enter* means to type a command and press Return to run it.

Examples

Examples show what should happen as you enter a command. Some examples assume that you've created certain files. If you haven't, you may not get the results shown.

We use typewriter-style characters for examples. In code samples, items you type to try the example are **boldface**. System messages and responses are constant width.

Here's an example:

```
% date
Mon Feb  4 16:17:25 PST 2002
%
```

The character % is the shell (system) prompt. To do this example, you would type date and then press Return. The date command responds "Mon Feb 4 16:17:25 PST 2002" and then returns you to the prompt.

Text you see in examples may not be exactly what you see on your screen. Different Unix versions have commands with different outputs. Sometimes we edit screen samples to eliminate distracting text or make them fit the page.

Problem Checklist

We've included problem checklists in some sections. You may skip these parts and go back to them if you have a problem.

Exercises

Some sections have exercises to reinforce the text you've read. Follow the exercises, but don't be afraid to experiment on your own.

Exercises have two columns. The lefthand column tells you what to do and the righthand column tells you how to do it. For example, a line in the section "Exercise: Entering a Few Commands" near the end of Chapter 1 shows the following:

Get today's date.   Enter date

To follow the exercise, type the word date on your keyboard and press the Return key. The lefthand column tells you what will happen.

After you try the commands, you'll have a better idea of the ones you want to learn more about. You can then get more information from the section "Documentation" in Chapter 10.

Comments and Questions

Please address any comments and questions concerning this book to the publisher:

O'Reilly & Associates, Inc.
1005 Gravenstein Highway North
Sebastopol, CA 95472
(800) 998-9938 (in the United States or Canada)
(707) 829-0515 (international or local)
(707) 829-0104 (fax)

To ask technical questions or comment on the book, send email to:

bookquestions@oreilly.com

We have a web site for the book where examples, errata, and any plans for future editions are listed. You can access this site at:

http://www.oreilly.com/catalog/lunixmacosx/

For more information about books, conferences, Resource Centers, and the O'Reilly Network, see the O'Reilly web site at:

http://www.oreilly.com

If you write to us, please include information about your Unix environment and the computer you use. You'll have our thanks, along with thanks from future readers of this handbook.

The Evolution of This Book

This book is based on the popular O'Reilly title *Learning the Unix Operating System*, by Jerry Peek, Grace Todino, and John Strang (currently in its fifth edition). There are many differences in this book to meet the needs of Mac OS X users, but the fundamental layout and explanations are the same.

Acknowledgments

I'd like to acknowledge the great work of Laurie Petrycki, the editor at O'Reilly, and the valuable information and review of the manuscript by Apple Computer, Inc. In addition, Justin Walker, Eugene Lee, David Mackler, and Adriaan Tijsseling offered helpful insight on the printer and sendmail configuration puzzles. I would also like to express my gratitude to Chuck Toporek and Chris Stone for their valuable comments on the draft manuscript. Thanks also to Christian Crumlish for his back-room assistance, and Tim O'Reilly for the opportunity to help revise the popular *Learning the Unix Operating System* book for the exciting new Mac OS X world. Oh, and a big grin to Linda, Ashley, and Gareth for letting me type, type, and type some more, ultimately getting this book out the door in a remarkably speedy manner.

## CHAPTER 1

Getting Started

With a typical Unix system, a staff person has to set up a Unix *account* for you before you can use it. With Mac OS X, however, every install automatically creates a default user account. The account is identified by your *username*, which is usually a single word or an abbreviation. Think of this account as your office—it's your personal place in the Unix environment.

When you log in to your OS X system, you're automatically logged into your Unix account as well. In fact, your Desktop and other customized features of your OS X environment have corresponding features in the Unix environment. Your files and programs can be accessed either through the Mac Finder or through a variety of Unix command-line utilities that you can reach from within OS X's Terminal window.

Working in the Unix Environment

To get into the Unix environment, launch the Terminal application. (That's Finder → Applications → Utilities → Terminal. If you expect to use the Terminal a lot, drag the Terminal icon from the Finder window onto the Dock. You can then launch Terminal with a single click.) Once Terminal is running, you'll see a window like the one in Figure 1-1.

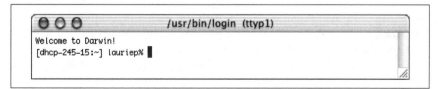

Figure 1-1. The Terminal window

Once you have a window open and you're typing commands, it's helpful to know that regular Mac OS X cut and paste commands work, so it's simple to send an email message to a colleague showing your latest Unix interaction, or to paste some text from a web page into a file you're editing with a Unix text editor such as vi.

You can also have a number of different Terminal windows open if that helps your workflow. Simply use ⌘-N to open each one, and ⌘-~ to cycle between them without removing your hands from the keyboard.

If you have material in your scroll buffer you want to find, use ⌘-F (select Find Panel from the Edit menu) and enter the specific text. ⌘-G (Find Next) lets you search down the scroll buffer for the next occurrence, and ⌘-D (Find Previous) lets you search up the scroll buffer for the previous occurrence. You can also accomplish this by highlighting a passage, entering ⌘-E (Enter Selection) and jumping to the selected material with ⌘-J (Jump to Selection). You can also save an entire Terminal session as a text file with File → Save, and you can print the entire session with File → Print. It's a good idea to study the key sequences shown in the Control menu, as illustrated in Figure 1-2.

Figure 1-2. Command sequences accessible from the Control menu

Inside the Terminal window, you're working with a program called a *shell*. The shell interprets command lines you enter, runs programs you ask for, and generally coordinates what happens between you and the Unix operating system. The default shell on OS X is called *tcsh*. Other available shells include the Bourne shell (*sh*), the C shell (*csh*), and the Z Shell (*zsh*). Popular shells on other versions of Unix (not available by default on OS X) include the Korn shell (*ksh*) and the Bourne-again shell (*bash*).

For a beginner, differences between shells are slight. If you plan to work with Unix a lot, though, you should learn more about your shell and its special commands.*

The Shell Prompt

When the system is ready to run a command, the shell outputs a *prompt* to tell you that you can enter a command.

The default prompt in *tcsh* is the computer name (which might be something automatically generated, such as dhcp-254-108, or a name you've given your system), the current directory (which might be represented by ~, Unix's shorthand for your home directory), your login name, and a percent sign. For example, the complete prompt might look like this: [limbo:~] taylor%. The prompt can be customized, though, so your own shell prompt may be different. We'll show you how to customize your prompt in Chapter 4.

A prompt that ends with a hash mark (#) usually means you're logged in as the *superuser*. The superuser doesn't have the protections for standard users that are built into the Unix system. If you don't know Unix well, you can inadvertently damage your system software when you are logged in as the superuser. In this case, we recommend that you stop work until you've found out how to access your personal Unix account.†

Entering a Command Line

Entering a command line at the shell prompt tells the computer what to do. Each command line includes the name of a Unix program. When you press Return, the shell interprets your command line and executes the program.

The first word that you type at a shell prompt is always a Unix command (or program name). Like most things in Unix, program names are case sensitive; if the program name is lowercase (and most are), you must type it in lowercase. Some simple command lines have just one word, which is the program name. For more information, see the section "Syntax of Unix Command Lines," later in this chapter.

---

* To find out which shell you're using, run the command echo $SHELL or ps $$. (See the section "Entering a Command Line," later in this chapter.) The answer, which could be something like */bin/tcsh*, is your shell's name or pathname. You can also look at Terminal → Preferences.

† This can happen if you're using a window system that was started by the superuser when the system was rebooted, or if your prompt has been customized to end with # when you aren't the superuser.

date

An example single-word command is date. Entering the command date displays the current date and time:

```
% date
Mon Feb  4 19:16:01 PST 2002
%
```

As you type a command line, the system simply collects your keyboard input. Pressing the Return key tells the shell that you've finished entering text, and it can run the program.

who

Another simple command is who. It displays a list of each logged-on user's username, terminal number, and login time. Try it now, if you'd like.

The who program can also tell you which account is currently using the Terminal application, in case you have multiple user accounts for yourself on your Mac. The command line for this is who am i. This command line consists of the command (who, the program's name) and arguments (am i). (Arguments are explained in the section "Syntax of Unix Command Lines" later in this chapter.) For example:

```
% who am i
taylor    ttyp1    Feb  4 16:16
```

The response shown in this example says that:

- "I am" Taylor (actually, my username is *taylor*). The username is the same as the Short Name you're asked to define when you create a new user with System Preferences → Users → New User. It can contain up to eight characters, and will always be shown in lowercase.

- I'm using terminal p1. (This cryptic syntax, ttyp1, is a holdover from the early days of Unix. All you need to know as a Unix beginner is that each time you open a new terminal window, the number at the end of the name gets incremented. The first one by ttyp1, the second ttyp2, and so on. The terminal ID also appears in the titlebar of the Terminal window.)

- I logged in (opened my Terminal window) at 4:16 in the afternoon of February 4.

Recalling Previous Commands

Modern Unix shells remember command lines you've typed previously. They can even remember commands from previous login sessions. This handy feature can save you a lot of retyping of common commands. As with many things in Unix, though, there are several different ways to do this; we don't have room to show and explain them all. You can get more information from sources listed in Chapter 10.

After you've typed and executed several command lines, try pressing the up-arrow key on your keyboard. You will see the previous command line after your shell prompt, just as you typed it before. Pressing the up arrow again recalls the previous command line, and so on. Also, as you'd expect, the down-arrow key will recall more recent command lines.

To execute one of these remembered commands, just press the Return key. (Your cursor doesn't have to be at the end of the command line.)

Once you've recalled a command line, you can edit it. If you don't want to execute any remembered commands, cancel the command line with Control-C or ⌘-.. The next section explains both of these.

Correcting a Command Line

What if you make a mistake in a command line? Suppose you typed dare instead of date and pressed the Return key before you realized your mistake. Most shells will give you an error message:

```
% dare
dare: command not found
%
```

The default shell in Mac OS X will try to guess what you meant in the same situation (note that you need to type y when it asks if date is the correct command to run):

```
% dare

OK? date? yes
Mon Feb  4 19:26:20 PST 2002
%
```

Don't be too concerned about getting error messages. Sometimes you'll get an error even if it appears that you typed the command correctly. This can be caused by typing control characters that are invisible on the screen. Once the prompt returns, reenter your command.

As we said earlier (in the section "Recalling Previous Commands"), most modern shells let you recall previous commands and edit command lines. If you plan to do a lot of work at the shell prompt, it's worth learning these handy techniques. They take more time to learn than we can spend here, though—except to mention that, on those shells, the left-arrow and right-arrow keys may move your cursor along the command line to the point where you want to make a change. Here, let's concentrate on simple methods that work with all shells.

If you see a mistake before you press Return, you can use the *erase character* to erase and correct the mistake.

The erase character differs between systems and accounts, and can be customized. The most common erase characters are:

- Delete or Del
- Control-H

Control-H is called a *control character*. To type a control character (for example, Control-H), hold down the Control key, then press the letter H. In the text, we write control characters as Control-H, but in the examples, we will use the standard Unix notation: ^H. This is not the same as pressing the ^ (caret) key, letting go, and then typing an H!

The Delete key may be used as the *interrupt character* instead of the erase character. This key is used to interrupt or cancel a command and can be used in many (but not all) cases when you want to quit what you're doing. Another character often programmed to do the same thing is Control-C, or ⌘..

Other common control characters are:

Control-U
Erases the whole input line; you can start over.

Control-S
Pauses output from a program that's writing to the screen. This can be confusing; we don't recommend using Control-S, but want you to be aware of it.

Control-Q
Restarts output after a Control-S pause.

Control-D
Signals the end of input for some programs (such as cat and mail, explained in the sections "Putting Text in a File" in Chapter 6 and "Electronic Mail" in Chapter 8, respectively) and returns you to a shell prompt. If you type Control-D at a shell prompt, it may close your current Terminal window.

Logging Out

To end a Unix session, you must log out. You should *not* end a session by just quitting the Terminal application or closing the terminal window. It's possible that you might have started a process running in the background (see Chapter 9), and closing the window will interrupt the process so it won't complete. Instead, type exit at a shell prompt. The window will either close or display Process Complete; then you can then safely quit the application. If you've started a background process, you'll instead get one of the messages in the Problem Checklist below.

Problem checklist

The first few times you use Unix, you aren't likely to have the following problems. But you may encounter these problems later, as you do more advanced work.

You get another shell prompt, or the shell says "logout: not login shell."
> You've been using a subshell (a shell created by your original login shell). To end each subshell, type exit (or just type Control-D) until you're logged out.

The shell says "There are stopped jobs" or "There are running jobs."
> Mac OS X and many other Unix systems have a feature called *job control* that lets you suspend a program temporarily while it's running or keep it running separately in the "background." One or more programs you ran during your session has not ended but is stopped (paused) or in the background. Enter fg to bring each stopped job into the foreground, then quit the program normally. (See Chapter 9 for more information.)

The Terminal application refuses to quit, saying "Quit: There are active windows."
> Terminal tries to help by not quitting when you're in the middle of running a command. Cancel the dialog box and make sure you don't have any commands running that you forgot about.

Syntax of Unix Command Lines

Unix command lines can be simple, one-word entries such as the date command. They can also be more complex; you may need to type more than the command or program name.[*]

A Unix command can have *arguments*. An argument can be an option or a filename. The general format for a Unix command line is:

```
command option(s) filename(s)
```

---

[*] The command can be the name of a Unix program (such as date), or it can be a command that's built into the shell (such as exit). You probably don't need to worry about this! You can read more precise definitions of these terms and others in the Glossary.

There isn't a single set of rules for writing Unix commands and arguments, but these general rules work in most cases:

- Enter commands in lowercase.

- *Options* modify the way in which a command works. Options are often single letters prefixed with a dash (-, also called "hyphen" or "minus") and set off by any number of spaces or tabs. Multiple options in one command line can be set off individually (such as -a -b). In some cases, you can combine them after a single dash (such as -ab), but most commands' documentation doesn't tell you whether this will work; you'll have to try it.

  Some commands also have options made from complete words or phrases and starting with two dashes, such as --delete or --confirm-delete. When you enter a command line, you can use this option style, the single-letter options (which each start with a single dash), or both.

- The argument *filename* is the name of a file you want to use. Most Unix programs also accept multiple filenames, separated by spaces or specified with wildcards (see Chapter 3). If you don't enter a filename correctly, you may get a response such as "*filename*: no such file or directory" or "*filename*: cannot open."

  Some commands, such as telnet and who (shown earlier in this chapter), have arguments that aren't filenames.

- You must type spaces between commands, options, and filenames. You'll need to "quote" filenames that contain spaces. For more information, see the section "File and Directory Names" in Chapter 3.

- Options come before filenames.

- In a few cases, an option has another argument associated with it; type this special argument just after its option. Most options don't work this way, but you should know about them. The sort command is an example of this feature: you can tell sort to write the sorted text to a filename given after its -o option. In the following example, sort reads the file *sortme* (given as an argument), and writes to the file *sorted* (given after the -o option):

  ```
  % sort -o sorted -n sortme
  ```

  We also used the -n option in that example. But -n is a more standard option; it has nothing to do with the final argument *sortme* on that command line. So, we also could have written the command line this way:

  ```
  % sort -n -o sorted sortme
  ```

Another example is the `mail -s` option, shown in the section "Sending Mail from a Shell Prompt" in Chapter 8. Don't be too concerned about these special cases, though. If a command needs an option like this, its documentation will say so.

- Command lines can have other special characters, some of which we see later in this book. They can also have several separate commands. For instance, you can write two or more commands on the same command line, each separated by a semicolon (`;`). Commands entered this way are executed one after another by the shell.

Unix has a lot of commands! Don't try to memorize all of them. In fact, you'll probably need to know just a few commands and their options. As time goes on, you'll learn these commands and the best way to use them for your job. We cover some useful Unix commands in later chapters. This book's quick reference card has quick reminders.

Let's look at a sample Unix command. The `ls` program displays a list of files. You can use it with or without options and arguments. If you enter:

```
% ls
```

you'll see a list of filenames. But if you enter:

```
% ls -l
```

there'll be an entire line of information for each file. The `-l` option (a dash and a lowercase letter "L") changes the normal `ls` output to a long format. You can also get information about a particular file by using its name as the second argument. For example, to find out about a file called *chap1*, enter:

```
% ls -l chap1
```

Many Unix commands have more than one option. For instance, `ls` has the `-a` (all) option for listing hidden files. You can use multiple options in either of these ways:

```
% ls -a -l
% ls -al
```

You must type one space between the command name and the dash that introduces the options. If you enter `ls-al`, the shell will say "ls-al: command not found."

Exercise: Entering a Few Commands

The best way to get used to Unix is to enter some commands. To run a command, type the command and then press the Return key. Remember that almost all Unix commands are typed in lowercase.

Here are a few to try:

Get today's date.	Enter date
List logged-in users.	Enter who
Obtain more information about users.	Enter who -u, finger, or w
Find out who is at your terminal.	Enter who am i
Enter two commands in the same line.	Enter who am i;date
Mistype a command.	Enter woh

In this session, you've tried several simple commands and seen the results on the screen.

Types of Commands

When you use a program, you'll want to know how to control it. How can you tell it what job you want done? Do you give instructions before the program starts, or after it's started? There are several general ways to give commands on a Unix system. It's good to be aware of them.

1. Some programs work only within the graphical window environment (on Mac OS X, this is called Aqua). On Mac OS X, you can run these programs using the open command. For instance, when you type open /Applications/Chess.app at a shell prompt, the chess game starts. It opens one or more windows on your screen. The program has its own way to receive your commands—through menus and buttons on its windows, for instance.

2. You've also seen in the section "Syntax of Unix Command Lines," that you can enter many Unix commands at a shell prompt. These programs work in a window system (from a terminal window) or from any terminal. You control those programs from the Unix command line—that is, by typing options and arguments from a shell prompt before you start the program. After you start the program, wait for it to finish; you generally don't interact with it.

3. Some Unix programs that work in the terminal window have commands of their own. (If you'd like some examples, see Chapters 2 and 3.) These programs may accept options and arguments on their command lines. But, once you start a program, it prints its own prompt and/or menus, and it understands its own commands; it takes instructions from your keyboard that weren't given on its command line.

   For instance, if you enter ftp at a shell prompt, you'll see a new prompt from the ftp program. Enter FTP commands to transfer files to and from remote systems. When you enter the special command quit to quit the ftp program, ftp will stop prompting you. Then you'll get another shell prompt, where you can enter other Unix commands.

The Unresponsive Terminal

During your Unix session, your terminal may not respond when you type a command, or the display on your screen may stop at an unusual place. That's called a "hung" or "frozen" terminal or session. Note that most of the techniques in this section apply to a terminal window, but not to non-terminal windows such as a web browser.

A session can hang for several reasons. For instance, your computer can get too busy; the Terminal application has to wait its turn. In that case, your session starts by itself after a few moments. You should *not* try to "un-hang" the session by entering extra commands, because those commands will all take effect after Terminal comes back to life.

If the system doesn't respond for quite a while (how long that is depends on your individual situation; ask other users about their experiences), the following solutions usually work. Try the following steps in the order shown until the system responds:

1. Press the Return key *once*.

   You may have typed text at a prompt (for example, a command line at a shell prompt) but haven't yet pressed Return to say that you're done typing and your text should be interpreted.

2. Try job control (see Chapter 9); type Control-Z.

   This control key sequence suspends a program that may be running and gives you a shell prompt. Now you can enter the jobs command to find the program's name, then restart the program with fg or terminate it with kill.

3. Use your interrupt key (found earlier in this chapter in "Correcting a Command Line"; typically Control-C).

   This interrupts a program that may be running. (Unless the program is run in the background, as described in the section, "Running a Command in the Background" in Chapter 9, the shell waits for it to finish before giving a new prompt. A long-running program may thus appear to hang the terminal.) If this doesn't work the first time, try it once more; doing it more than twice usually won't help.

4. Type Control-Q.

   If output has been stopped with Control-S, this will restart it. (Note that some systems will automatically issue Control-S if they need to pause output; this character may not have been typed from the keyboard.)

5. Type Control-D *once* at the beginning of a new line.

   Some programs (such as mail) expect text from the user. A program may be waiting for an end-of-input character from you to tell it that you've finished entering text. Typing Control-D may cause you to log out, so you should try this only as a last resort.

6. Otherwise, quit your Terminal application and start it up again.

## CHAPTER 2

Using Unix

Once you launch Terminal, you can use the many facilities that Unix provides. As an authorized system user, you have an account that gives you:

- A place in the Unix filesystem where you can store your files.
- A username that identifies you, lets you control access to your files, and is an address for your email (although it may not be your main address).
- An environment you can customize.

The Unix Filesystem

A *file* is the unit of storage in Unix, as it is in the Mac environment. A file can hold anything: text (a report you're writing, a to-do list), a program, digitally encoded pictures or sound, and so on. All of those are just sequences of raw data until they're interpreted by the right program.

In Unix, files are organized into directories. A *directory* is actually a special kind of file where the system stores information about other files. (A Unix directory is identical to a Mac folder.) You can think of a directory as a place, so that files are said to be contained *in* directories, and you work *inside* a directory.

This section introduces the Unix filesystem. Later sections show how you can look in files and protect them. Chapter 3 has more information.

Your Home Directory

When you launch Terminal, you're placed in a directory called your *home directory*. This directory, a unique place in the Mac OS X filesystem, contains the files you use almost every time you log in. In your home directory, you can create your own files. As you'll see, you can also store your own directories within your home directory. Like folders in a file cabinet, this is a good way to organize your files.

Your Working Directory

Your *working directory* (also called your current directory) is the directory in which you're currently working. Every time you launch Terminal, your home directory is your working directory. When you change to another directory, the directory you move to becomes your working directory.

Unless you tell Unix otherwise, all commands that you enter apply to the files in your working directory. In the same way, when you create files, they're created in your working directory unless you specify another directory. For instance, if you type the command vi report, the vi editor is started, and a file named *report* is created in your working directory. But if you type a command such as vi /Users/john/report, a *report* file is edited in a different directory—without changing your working directory. You'll learn more about this when we cover pathnames later in this chapter.

If you have more than one Terminal window open, each session has its own working directory. Changing the working directory in one session doesn't affect other Terminal windows.

The Directory Tree

All directories on a Unix system are organized into a hierarchical structure that you can imagine as a family tree. The parent directory of the tree (the directory that contains all other directories) is known as the *root directory* and is written as a forward slash (/).

The root contains several directories. Figure 2-1 shows a visual representation of the top of a Unix filesystem tree: the root directory and some directories under the root.

bin, *etc*, *users*, *tmp*, and *usr* are some of the *subdirectories* (child directories) of the root directory. These subdirectories are fairly standard; they usually contain specific XML (Extensible Markup Language) option (spelling)kinds of system files. For instance, *bin* contains many Unix programs.

In our example, the parent directory of *Users* (one level above) is the root directory. It has two subdirectories (one level below), *john* and *carol*. On a Mac OS X system, each directory has only one parent directory, but it may have one or more subdirectories.*

---

* On most Unix systems, including Mac OS X, the root directory at the top of the tree is *its own* parent.

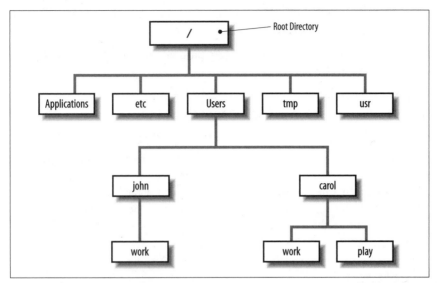

Figure 2-1. Example of a directory tree

A subdirectory (such as *carol*) can have its own subdirectories (such as *work* and *play*). The number of subdirectories is limited, though users will probably never reach that limit.

To specify a file or directory location, write its *pathname*. A pathname is like the address of the directory or file in the Unix filesystem. We look at pathnames in the next section.

On a basic Unix system, all files in the filesystem are stored on disks connected to your computer. It isn't always easy to use the files on someone else's computer or for someone on another computer to use your files. Your system may have an easier way: a *networked filesystem*. Networked filesystems make a remote computer's files appear as if they're part of your computer's directory tree. For instance, a computer in Los Angeles might have a directory named *boston* with some of the directory tree from a company's computer in Boston. Or individual users' home directories may come from various computers, but all be available on your computer as if they were local files. Your Mac admin can help you understand and configure your computer's filesystems to make your work easier.

Absolute Pathnames

As you saw earlier, the Unix filesystem organizes its files and directories in an inverted tree structure with the root directory at the top. An *absolute pathname* tells you the path of directories through which you must travel to get from the root to the directory or file you want. In a pathname, put slashes (/) between the directory names.

For example, */Users/john* is an absolute pathname. It locates one (*only* one!) directory. Here's how:

- The root is the first slash (/).
- The directory *Users* (a subdirectory of *root*) is second.
- The directory *john* (a subdirectory of *Users*) is last.

Be sure that you do not type spaces anywhere in the pathname. If there are spaces in one or more of the directories, you need to either quote the entire directory pathname, or preface each space with a backslash to ensure that the shell understands that the spaces are part of the pathname itself. Figure 2-2 shows this structure.

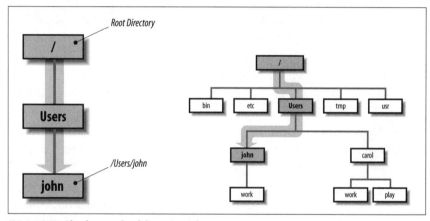

Figure 2-2. Absolute path of directory john

In Figure 2-2, you'll see that the directory *john* has a subdirectory named *work*. Its absolute pathname is */Users/john/work*.

The root is always indicated by the slash (/) at the start of the pathname. In other words, an absolute pathname always starts with a slash.

Relative Pathnames

You can also locate a file or directory with a *relative pathname*. A relative pathname gives the location relative to your working directory.

Unless you use an absolute pathname (starting with a slash), Unix assumes that you're using a relative pathname. Like absolute pathnames, relative pathnames can go through more than one directory level by naming the directories along the path.

For example, if you're currently in the *Users* directory (see Figure 2-2), the relative pathname to the *carol* directory below is simply *carol*. The relative pathname to the *play* directory below that is *carol/play*.

Notice that neither pathname in the previous paragraph starts with a slash. That's what makes them relative pathnames! Relative pathnames start at the working directory, not the root directory. In other words, a relative pathname never starts with a slash.

Pathname puzzle

Here's a short but important question. The previous example explains the relative pathname *carol/play*. What do you think Unix would say about the pathname */carol/play*? (Look again at Figure 2-2.)

Unix would say "No such file or directory." Why? (Please think about that before you read more. It's very important and it's one of the most common beginner's mistakes.) Here's the answer. Because it starts with a slash, the pathname */carol/play* is an absolute pathname that starts from the root. It says to look in the root directory for a subdirectory named *carol*. But there is no subdirectory named *carol* one level directly below the root, so the pathname is wrong. The only absolute pathname to the *play* directory is */Users/carol/play*.

Relative pathnames up

You can go up the tree with the shorthand .. (dot dot) for the parent directory. As you saw earlier, you can also go down the tree by using subdirectory names. In either case (up or down), separate each level by a / (slash).

Figure 2-3 shows part of Figure 2-1. If your working directory in the figure is *work*, then there are two pathnames for the *play* subdirectory of *carol*. You already know how to write the absolute pathname, */Users/carol/play*. You can also go up one level (with ..) to *carol*, then go down the tree to *play*. Figure 2-3 illustrates this.

The relative pathname would be *../play*. It would be wrong to give the relative address as *carol/play*. Using *carol/play* would say that *carol* is a subdirectory of your working directory instead of what it is in this case: the parent directory.

Absolute and relative pathnames are interchangeable. Unix programs simply follow whichever path you specify to wherever it leads. If you use an absolute pathname, the path starts from the root. If you use a relative pathname, the path starts from your working directory. Choose whichever is easier at the moment.

Figure 2-3. Relative pathname from work to play

Changing Your Working Directory

Once you know the absolute or relative pathname of a directory where you'd like to work, you can move up and down the Unix directory tree to reach it. The following sections explain some helpful commands for navigating through a directory tree.

pwd

To find which directory you're currently in, use pwd (print working directory), which prints the absolute pathname of your working directory. The pwd command takes no arguments.

```
% pwd
/Users/john
%
```

cd

You can change your working directory to any directory (including another user's directory, if you have permission) with the cd (change directory) command, which has the form:

```
cd pathname
```

The argument is an absolute or a relative pathname (whichever is easier) for the directory you want to change to:

```
% cd /Users/carol
% pwd
/Users/carol
% cd work
% pwd
/Users/carol/work
%
```

The command cd, with no arguments, takes you to your home directory from wherever you are in the filesystem.

Note that you can only change to another directory. You cannot cd to a filename. If you try, your shell (in this example, *tcsh*) gives you an error message:

```
% cd /etc/man.conf
/etc/man.conf:  Not a directory.
%
```

/etc/man.conf is a file with information about the configuration of the man command.

One neat trick worth mentioning is that you can always have Terminal enter the path directly by dragging a file or folder icon from the Finder onto the active Terminal window.

Two Ways to Explore Your Filesystem

Every file and folder that you view from the Finder is also accessible from the Unix shell. Changes made in one environment are reflected (almost) immediately in the other. For example, the Desktop folder is also the Unix directory */Users/yourname/Desktop*.

Just for fun, open a Finder window, move to your *Desktop* folder, and keep it visible while you type these commands at the shell prompt:

```
% cd
% cd Desktop
% touch mac-rocks
```

Watch a file called *mac-rocks* appear magically on the Desktop. (The touch command creates an empty file with the name you specify.)

Now type:

```
% rm mac-rocks
```

and watch the file disappear. The rm command removes the file.

Files in the Directory Tree

A directory can hold subdirectories. And, of course, a directory can hold files. Figure 2-4 is a close-up of the filesystem around *john*'s home directory. The four files are shown along with the *work* subdirectory.

Pathnames to files are made the same way as pathnames to directories. As with directories, files' pathnames can be absolute (starting from the root

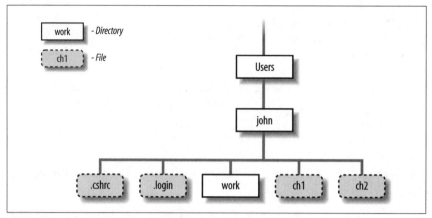

Figure 2-4. Files in the directory tree

directory) or relative (starting from the working directory). For example, if your working directory is *Users*, the relative pathname to the *work* directory below would be *john/work*. The relative pathname to the *ch1* file would be *john/ch1*.

Unix filesystems can hold things that aren't directories or files, such as symbolic links, FIFOs, and sockets (they have pathnames, too). You may see some of them as you explore the filesystem. We don't cover those advanced topics in this little book.

Listing Files with ls

To use the `cd` command, you must know which entries in a directory are subdirectories and which are files. The `ls` command lists entries in the directory tree and can also show you which is which.

When you enter the `ls` command, you get a list of the files and subdirectories contained in your working directory. The syntax is:

```
ls option(s) directory-and-filename(s)
```

If you've just moved into an empty directory, entering ls without any arguments may seem to do nothing. This isn't surprising, because you haven't made any files in your working directory. If you have no files, nothing is displayed; you'll simply get a new shell prompt:

```
% ls
%
```

But if you're in your home directory, ls displays the names of the files and directories in that directory. The output depends on what's in your directory. The screen should look something like this:

```
% ls
Desktop    Documents   Library   Movies   Music   Pictures   Public
%
```

Sometimes ls might display filenames in a single column. If yours does, you can make a multicolumn display with the -C (uppercase "C") option or the -x option. ls has a lot of options that change the information and display format.

The -a option (for all) is guaranteed to show you some more files, as in the following example, which shows a directory like the one in Figure 2-4:

```
% ls -a
.                           .Trash      .bash_history   .bashrc
.tcsh_history Desktop       Documents   Library         Movies
Music         Pictures      Public
%
```

When you use ls -a, you'll always see at least two entries with the names . (dot) and .. (dot dot). As mentioned earlier, .. is always the relative pathname to the parent directory. A single . always stands for its working directory; this is useful with commands such as cp (see the section "Copying Files" in Chapter 3). There may also be other files, such as *.tcshr* or *.exrc*. Any entry whose name begins with a dot is hidden—it's listed only if you use ls -a.

To get more information about each item that ls lists, add the -l option. (That's a lowercase "L" for "long.") This option can be used alone, or in combination with -a, as shown in Figure 2-5.

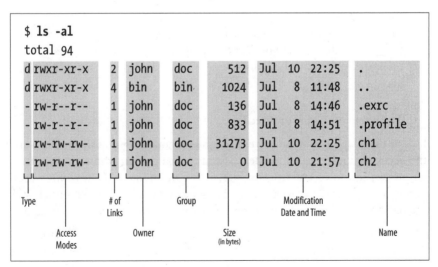

Figure 2-5. Output from ls -al

The long format provides the following information about each item:

Total n
> *n* is the amount of storage used by everything in this directory. (This is measured in *blocks*.) On Mac OS X, blocks are 1,024 bytes in size.

Type
> Tells whether the item is a directory (d) or a plain file (-). (There are other less common types that we don't explain here.)

Access modes
> Specifies three types of users (yourself, your group, all others) who are allowed to read (r), write (w), or execute (x) your files or directories. We'll talk more about access modes later.

Links
> The number of files or directories linked to this one. (This isn't the same as a web page link. We don't discuss filesystem links in this little book.)

Owner
> The user who created or owns this file or directory.

Group
> The group that owns the file or directory.

Size (in bytes)
> The size of the file or directory. (A directory is actually a special type of file. Here, the "size" of a directory is of the directory file itself, not the total of all the files in that directory.)

Modification date
> The date when the file was last modified, or when the directory contents last changed (when something in the directory was added, renamed, or removed). If an entry was modified more than six months ago, ls shows the year instead of the time.

Name
> The name of the file or directory.

Notice especially the columns that list the owner and group of the files, and the access modes (also called permissions). The person who creates a file is its owner; if you've created any files, this column should show your username. You also belong to a group. Files you create are marked either with the name of your group or, in some cases, the group that owns the directory.

The permissions show who can read, write, or execute the file or directory. The permissions have 10 characters. The first character shows the file type (d for directory or - for a plain file). The other characters come in groups of three. The first group, characters 2–4, shows the permissions for the file's owner, which is you if you created the file. The second group, characters 5–7, shows permissions for other members of the file's group. The third group, characters 8–10, shows permissions for all other users.

For example, the permissions for .*profile* in Figure 2-5 are -rw-r--r--, so it's a plain file. The owner, *john*, has both read and write permissions. Other users who belong to the file's group *doc*, as well as all other users of the system, can only read the file; they don't have write permission, so they can't change what's in the file. No one has execute (x) permission, which should be used only for executable files (programs).

In the case of directories, x means the permission to access the directory—for example, to run a command that reads a file there or to use a subdirectory. Notice that the two directories shown in Figure 2-5 are executable (accessible) by *john*, by users in the *doc* group, and by everyone else on the system. A directory with write (w) permission allows deleting, renaming, or adding files within the directory. Read (r) permission allows listing the directory with ls.

You can use the chmod command to change the permissions of your files and directories. (See the section "Protecting and Sharing Files" later in this chapter.) If you need to know only which files are directories and which are executable files, you can use the -F option with ls.

If you give the pathname to a directory, ls lists the directory but does *not* change your working directory. The pwd command here shows this:

```
% ls -F /Users/andy
calendar    goals    ideas/
ch2         guide/   testpgm*
% pwd
/Applications
%
```

ls -F puts a / (slash) at the end of each directory name. (The directory name doesn't really have a slash in it; that's just the shorthand ls -F uses to identify a directory.) In our example, *guide* and *ideas* are directories. You can verify this by using ls -l and noting the d in the first field of the output. Files with an execute status (x), such as programs, are marked with an * (asterisk). The file *testpgm* is an executable file. Files that aren't marked are not executable.

ls -R (recursive) lists a directory and all its subdirectories. This can make a very long list—especially when you list a directory near the root! (Piping the output of ls to a pager program solves this problem. There's an example in the section "Piping to a Pager.") You can combine other options with -R; for instance, ls -RF marks each directory and file type, while recursively listing files and directories.

On Mac OS X systems that include the GNU version of ls (perhaps from *http://www.gnu.org*), you may be able to see names in color. For instance, directories could be green and program files could be yellow. Like almost everything on Unix, of course, this is configurable. The details are more than we can cover in an introductory book. Try typing ls --color and see what happens. (It's time for our familiar mantra: check your documentation. See the section "Where to Go from Here." The man command is especially useful for reading a command's online manual page.)

Exercise: Exploring the Filesystem

You're now equipped to explore the filesystem with cd, ls, and pwd. Take a tour of the directory system, hopping one or many levels at a time, with a mixture of cd and pwd commands.

Go to your home directory.	Enter cd
Find your working directory.	Enter pwd
Change to new working directory with its absolute pathname.	Enter cd /bin
List files in new working directory.	Enter ls
Change directory to root and list it in one step. (Use the command separator: a semicolon.)	Enter cd /; ls
Find your working directory.	Enter pwd
Change to a subdirectory; use its relative pathname.	Enter cd usr
Find your working directory.	Enter pwd
Change to a subdirectory.	Enter cd lib
Find your working directory.	Enter pwd
Give a wrong pathname.	Enter cd xqk
List files in another directory.	Enter ls /bin
Find your working directory (notice that ls didn't change it).	Enter pwd
Return to your home directory.	Enter cd

Looking Inside Files with less

By now, you're probably tired of looking at files from the outside. It's akin to visiting a bookstore and looking at the covers, but never getting to read a word. Let's look at a program for reading text files.

If you want to "read" a long file on the screen, you can use the less command to display one "page" (a Terminal window filled from top to bottom) of text at a time.

If you don't like less, you can try a very similar program named more. (In fact, the name less is a play on the name of more, which came first.) The syntax for less is:

```
less option(s) file(s)
```

less lets you move forward or backward in the files by any number of pages or lines; you can also move back and forth between two or more files specified on the command line. When you invoke less, the first "page" of the file appears. A prompt appears at the bottom of the Terminal window, as in the following example:

```
% less ch03
A file is the unit of storage in Unix, as in most other systems.
A file can hold anything: text (a report you're writing,
   .
   .
   .
   :
```

The basic less prompt is a colon (:); although, for the first screenful, less displays the file's name as a prompt. The cursor sits to the right of this prompt as a signal for you to enter a less command to tell less what to do. To quit, type q.

Like almost everything about less, the prompt can be customized. For example, using the -M starting flag on the less command line makes the prompt show the filename and your position in the file (as a percentage). If you want this to happen every time you use less, you can set the LESS environment variable to M (without a dash) in your shell setup file. See the section "Customizing Your Shell Environment" in Chapter 4.

You can set or unset most options temporarily from the less prompt. For instance, if you have the short less prompt (a colon), you can enter -M while less is running. less responds "Long prompt (press Return)," and for the rest of the session, less prompts with the filename, line number, and percentage of the file viewed.

To display the less commands and options available on your system, press h (for "help") while less is running. Table 2-1 lists some simple (but still quite useful) commands.

Table 2-1. Useful less commands

Command	Description	Command	Description
SPACE	Display next page.	v	starts the vi editor
Return	Display next line.	Control-L	Redisplay current page.
nf	Move forward n lines.	h	Help.
b	Move backward one page.	:n	Go to next file on command line.
nb	Move backward n lines.	:p	Go back to previous file on command line.
/word	Search forward for word.		
?word	Search backward for word.	q	Quit less.

Protecting and Sharing Files

Unix makes it easy for users on the same system to share files and directories. For instance, everyone in a group can read documents stored in one of their manager's directories without needing to make their own copies, if the manager has allowed access. There might be no need to fill peoples' email inboxes with file attachments if everyone can access those files directly through the Unix filesystem.

Here's a brief introduction to file security and sharing. If you have critical security needs, or you just want more information, talk to your system staff or see an up-to-date book on Unix security such as *Practical Unix and Internet Security* (O'Reilly).

 Note that the system's superuser (the system administrator and possibly other users) can do anything to any file at any time, no matter what its permissions are. So, access permissions won't keep your private information safe from *everyone*—although let's hope that you can trust your system administrator!

Your system administrator should also keep backup copies of users' files. These backup copies may be readable by anyone who has physical access to them. That is, anyone who can take the backup out of a cabinet (or wherever) and mount it on a computer system may be able to read the file copies. The same is true for files stored on floppy disks and any other removable media. (Once you take a file off a Unix system, that system can't control access to it anymore.)

Directory Access Permissions

A directory's access permissions help to control access to the files and subdirectories in that directory:

- If a directory has read permission, a user can run ls to see what's in the directory and use wildcards to match files in it.

- A directory that has write permission allows users to add, rename, and delete files in the directory.

- To access a directory (that is, to read or write the files in the directory or to run the files if they're programs) a user needs execute permission on that directory. Note that to access a directory, a user must *also* have execute permission to all its parent directories, all the way up to the root.

File Access Permissions

The access permissions on a file control what can be done to the file's *contents*. The access permissions on the directory where the file is kept control whether the file can be renamed or removed. (If this seems confusing, think of it this way: the directory is actually a list of files. Adding, renaming, or removing a file changes the contents of the directory. If the directory isn't writable, you can't change that list.)

Read permission controls whether you can read a file's contents. Write permission lets you change a file's contents. A file shouldn't have execute permission unless it's a program.

Setting Permissions with chmod

Once you know what permissions a file or directory needs—and if you're the owner (listed in the third column of `ls -l` output)—you can change the permissions with the chmod program.

There are two ways to change permissions: by specifying the permissions to add or delete, or by specifying the exact permissions. For instance, if a directory's permissions are almost correct, but you also need to make it writable by its group, tell chmod to add group-write permission. But if you need to make more than one change to the permissions—for instance, if you want to add read and execute permission but delete write permission—it's easier to set all permissions explicitly instead of changing them one-by-one. The syntax is:

```
chmod permissions file(s)
```

Let's start with the rules; we see examples next. The *permissions* argument has three parts, which you must give in order with no space between.

1. The category of permission you want to change. There are three: the owner's permission (which chmod calls "user," abbreviated u), the group's permission (g), or others' permission (o). To change more than one category, string the letters together, such as go for "group and others," or simply use a to mean "all" (same as ugo).

2. Whether you want to add (+) the permission, delete (-) it, or specify it exactly (=).

3. What permissions you want to affect: read (r), write (w), or execute (x). To change more than one permission, string the letters together—for example, rw for "read and write."

Some examples should make this clearer! In the following command lines, you can replace *dirname* or *filename* with the pathname (absolute or relative) of the directory or file. An easy way to change permissions on the working directory is by using its relative pathname, . (dot), as in chmod a-w .. You can combine two permission changes in the same chmod command by separating them with a comma (,), as shown in the final example.

- To protect a file from accidental editing, delete everyone's write permission with the command chmod a-w *filename*. On the other hand, if you own an unwritable file that you want to edit, but you don't want to change other peoples' write permissions, you can add "user" (owner) write permission with chmod u+w *filename*.

- To keep yourself from accidentally removing files (or adding or renaming files) in an important directory of yours, delete your own write permission with the command chmod u-w *dirname*. If other users have that permission too, you could delete everyone's write permission with chmod a-w *dirname*.

- If you want you and your group to be able to read and write all the files in your working directory—but those files have various permissions now, so adding and deleting the permissions individually would be a pain—this is a good place to use the = operator to set the exact permissions you want. Use the filename wildcard *, which means "everything in this directory" (explained in the section "File and Directory Wildcards") and type: chmod ug=rw *.

- If your working directory had any subdirectories, though, that command would be wrong because it takes away execute permission from the subdirectories, so the subdirectories couldn't be accessed anymore. In that case, you could try a more specific wildcard. Or, instead of a wildcard, you can simply list the filenames you want to change, separated by spaces, as in chmod ug=rw afile bfile cfile.

- To protect the files in a directory and all its subdirectories from everyone else on your system, but still keep the access permissions *you* have there, you could use chmod go-rwx *dirname* to delete all "group" and "others" permission to read, write, and execute. A simpler way is to use the command chmod go= *dirname* to set "group" and "others" permission to exactly nothing.

- You want full access to a directory. Other people on the system should be able to see what's in the directory (and read or edit the files if the file permissions allow it) but not rename, remove, or add files. To do that, give yourself all permissions, but give "group" and "others" only read and execute permission. Use the command chmod u=rwx,go=rx *dirname*.

After you change permissions, it's a good idea to check your work with `ls -l` *filename* or `ls -ld` *dirname*.

Problem checklist

I get the message "chmod: Not owner."

> Only the owner of a file or directory (or the superuser) can set its permissions. Use `ls -l` to find the owner or ask a system administrator to change the permissions.

A file is writable, but my program says it can't be written.

> First, check the file permissions with `ls -l` and be sure you're in the category (user, group, or others) that has write permission.

> The problem may also be in the permissions of the file's directory. Some programs need permission to write more files into the same directory (for example, temporary files), or to rename files (for instance, making a file into a backup) while editing. If it's safe to add write permission to the directory (if other files in the directory don't need protection from removal or renaming) try that. Otherwise, copy the file to a writable directory (with `cp`), edit it there, then copy it back to the original directory.

Changing Group and Owner

Group ownership lets a certain group of users have access to a file or directory. You might need to let a different group have access. The `chgrp` program sets the group owner of a file or directory. You can set the group to any of the groups to which you belong. Because you're likely going to be administering your system, you can control the list of groups you're in. (In some situations, the system administrator controls the list of groups you're in.) The `groups` program lists your groups.

For example, if you're a designer creating a directory named *images* for several illustrators, the directory's original group owner might be *managers*. You'd like the illustrators, all of whom are in the group named *staff*, to access the directory; members of other groups should have no access. Use commands such as:[*]

```
% groups
managers staff freelancers research
% mkdir images
% ls -ld images
```

---

[*] Many Unix systems also let you set a directory's group ownership so that any files you later create in that directory will be owned by the same group as the directory. Try the command `chmod g+s` *dirname*. The permissions listing from `ls -ld` will now show an *s* in place of the second x, such as drwxr-s---.

```
drwxr-xr-x    2 roberts   managers      4096 Aug 25 13:35 images
% chgrp staff images
% chmod o= images
% ls -ld images
drwxr-x---    2 roberts   staff      4096 Aug 25 13:35 images
```

The chown program changes the owner of a file or directory. Mac OS X lets you reassign file and directory owners to your heart's content. On some other Unix systems, only the superuser can use chown.* You do have to be the original owner, however, so there are still some limitations.

Changing Your Password

The ownership and permissions system described in this chapter depends on the security of your username and password. If others get your username and password, they can log into your account and do anything you can. They can read private information, corrupt or delete important files, send email messages as if they came from you, and more. If your computer is connected to a network, whether it be the Internet or a local network inside your organization, intruders may also be able to log in without sitting at your keyboard! See the section "Remote Logins" in Chapter 7 for one way this can be done.

Anyone may be able to get your username—it's usually part of your email address, for instance, or shows up as a file's owner in a long directory listing. Your password is what keeps others from logging in as you. Don't leave your password anywhere around your computer. Don't give your password to anyone who asks you for it unless you're sure he'll preserve your account security. Also don't send your password by email; it can be stored, unprotected, on other systems and on backup tapes, where other people may find it and then break into your account.

If you think that someone knows your password, you should probably change it right away—although if you suspect that a computer "cracker" (or "hacker") is using your account to break into your system, you should ask your system administrator for advice first, if possible. You should also change your password periodically. Every few months is recommended.

A password should be easy for you to remember but hard for other people (or password-guessing programs) to guess. Here are some guidelines. A password should be between six and eight characters long. It should not be a word in any language, a proper name, your phone number, your address,

---

* If you have permission to read another user's file, you can make a copy of it (with cp; see the section "Copying Files" in Chapter 3). You'll own the copy.

---

or anything anyone else might know or guess that you'd use as a password. It's best to mix upper- and lowercase letters, punctuation, and numbers. A good way to come up with a unique but memorable password is to think of a phrase that only you might know, and use the first letters of each word (and punctuation) to create the password. For example, consider the password mlwsiF! ("My laptop was stolen in Florence!").

To change your password, you can use System Preferences → Users, but you can also change it from the command line using the `passwd` command. After you enter the command, it prompts you to enter your old password. If the password is correct, it asks you to enter the new password—twice, to be sure there is no typing mistake. For security, neither the old nor the new passwords appear as you type them.

Graphical Filesystem Browsers

Because you've the luxury of running Unix within the Mac OS X environment, there's also a terrific graphical way to do some of the things you can do with files from the command line. A *filesystem browser*, such as the Finder, lets you see a graphical representation of the filesystem and do a limited number of operations on it. Figure 2-6 shows the Finder in its default icon view. Other views that are helpful are listing and directory views, each offering more information about the directories above and below the current directory.

Figure 2-6. Mac OS X Finder, icon view

The Finder can be handy for seeing what's in the filesystem. Unfortunately, because the Finder takes you away from the shell you're using for other work, it can limit what you're able to do with Unix. (You'll see additional information about why this is true when we cover more advanced features such as input/output redirection in Chapter 6.) We recommend learning more about the Finder, but also learning what you can do at the more powerful Unix command line.

Completing File and Directory Names

Most Unix shells can complete a partly typed file or directory name for you. Different shells have different methods. If you're using the default shell in Mac OS X, *tcsh*, just type the first few letters of the name, then press Tab. If the shell can find just one way to finish the name, it will; your cursor will move to the end of the new name, where you can type more or press Return to run the command. (You can also edit or erase the completed name.)

What happens if more than one file or directory name matches what you've typed so far? You will get a list of all possible completions; try pressing Tab and you may see a list of all names starting with the characters you've typed so far. Here's an example from the *tcsh* shell:

```
% maTab
mach_init    mailq        make         makemap        man
machine      mailstat     makedbm      makepsres
mail         mailstats    makedepend   malloc_history
% ma
```

At this point, you could type another character or two—an i, for example— and then press Tab once more to list only the mail-related commands.

## CHAPTER 3

File Management

Chapter 2 introduced the Unix filesystem. This chapter explains how to name, edit, copy, move, and find files.

File and Directory Names

As Chapter 2 explains, both files and directories are identified by their names. A directory is really just a special kind of file, so the rules for naming directories are the same as the rules for naming files.

Filenames may contain any character except /, which is reserved as the separator between files and directories in a pathname. Filenames are usually made of upper- and lowercase letters, numbers, "." (dots), and "_" (underscores). Other characters (including spaces) are legal in a filename, but they can be hard to use because the shell gives them special meanings. However, spaces are a standard part of Macintosh file and folder names, so while we recommend using only letters, numbers, dots, and underscore characters for filenames, the reality is that you will have to figure out how to work with the spaces in file and directory names. The Finder, by contrast, dislikes colons (which it uses as a directory separator, just as Unix uses the slash). If you display a file called *test:me* in the Finder, the name is shown as *test/me* instead.

If you have a file with spaces in its name, the shell will be confused if you type its name on the command line. That's because the shell breaks command lines into separate arguments at the spaces. To tell the shell not to break an argument at spaces, either put quotation marks (") around the argument or preface each space with a backslash (\).

For example, the rm program, covered later in this chapter, removes Unix files. To remove a file named *a confusing name*, the first rm command in the following snippet doesn't work, but the second one does. Also note that you can escape spaces (that is, avoid having the shell interpret them inappropriately) by using a backslash character, as shown in the third example:

```
% ls -l
total 2
-rw-r--r--  1 taylor  staff   324 Feb  4 23:07 a confusing name
-rw-r--r--  1 taylor  staff    64 Feb  4 23:07 another odd name
% rm a confusing name
rm: a: no such file or directory
rm: confusing: no such file or directory
rm: name: no such file or directory
% rm "a confusing name"
% rm another\ odd\ name
%
```

Unix doesn't require a dot (.) in a filename; in fact, you can use as many as you want. For instance, the filenames *pizza* and *this.is.a.mess* are both legal. One interesting quirk of Mac OS X is that the colon is used in the graphical interface (Aqua) to separate folders and filenames, so it can't be used as part of a filename in the Finder. However, Unix doesn't care and is perfectly fine creating a file named *test:file*. When viewed in the Finder, however, it's displayed as *test/file* and vice versa.

A filename must be unique inside its directory, but other directories may have files with the same names. For example, you may have the files called *chap1* and *chap2* in the directory */Users/carol/work* and also have files with the same names in */Users/carol/play*.

File and Directory Wildcards

When you have a number of files named in series (for example, *chap1* to *chap12*) or filenames with common characters (such as *aegis*, *aeon*, and *aerie*), you can use wildcards to specify many files at once. These special characters are * (asterisk), ? (question mark), and [ ] (square brackets). When used in a file or directory name given as an argument on a command line, the following is true:

* An asterisk stands for any number of characters in a filename. For example, ae* would match *aegis*, *aerie*, *aeon*, etc. if those files were in the same directory. You can use this to save typing for a single filename (for example, al* for *alphabet.txt*) or to choose many files at once (as in ae*). A * by itself matches all file and subdirectory names in a directory, with the exception of any starting with a period. To match all your dot files, try .??*.

? A question mark stands for any single character (so h?p matches *hop* and *hip*, but not *help*).

[] Square brackets can surround a choice of single characters (i.e., one digit or one letter) you'd like to match. For example, [Cc]hapter would match either *Chapter* or *chapter*, but chap[12] would match *chap1* or *chap2*. Use a hyphen (-) to separate a range of consecutive characters. For example, chap[1-3] would match *chap1*, *chap2*, or *chap3*.

The following examples show the use of wildcards. The first command lists all the entries in a directory, and the rest use wildcards to list just some of the entries. The last one is a little tricky; it matches files whose names contain two (or more) *a*'s.

```
% ls
chap10        chap2        chap5      cold
chap1a.old    chap3.old    chap6      haha
chap1b        chap4        chap7      oldjunk
% ls chap?
chap2    chap5    chap7
chap4    chap6
% ls chap[5-7]
chap5    chap6    chap7
% ls chap[5-9]
chap5    chap6    chap7
% ls chap??
chap10   chap1b
% ls *old
chap1a.old    chap3.old    cold
% ls *a*a*
chap1a.old    haha
```

Wildcards are useful for more than listing files. Most Unix programs accept more than one filename, and you can use wildcards to name multiple files on the command line. For example, both the cat and less programs display files on the screen. cat streams a file's contents until end of file, while less shows the file one screenful at a time. Let's say you want to display files *chap3.old* and *chap1a.old*. Instead of specifying these files individually, you could enter the command as:

```
% less *.old
```

This is equivalent to less chap1a.old chap3.old.

Wildcards match directory names, too. You can use them anywhere in a pathname—absolute or relative—though you still need to separate directory levels with slashes (/). For example, let's say you have subdirectories named *Jan*, *Feb*, *Mar*, and so on. Each has a file named *summary*. You could read all the summary files by typing less */summary. That's almost equivalent to less Jan/summary Feb/summary ... but there's one important difference: the names will be alphabetized, so *Apr/summary* would be first in the list.

Creating and Editing Files

One easy way to create a file is with a Unix feature called *input/output redirection*, as Chapter 5 explains. This sends the output of a program directly to a file, to make a new file or add to an existing one.

You'll usually create and edit a plain-text file with a text editor program. Text editors are somewhat different than word processors.

Text Editors and Word Processors

A text editor lets you add, change, and rearrange text easily. Three popular Unix editors included with Mac OS X are *vi* (pronounced "vee-eye"), *Pico* ("pea-co"), and *Emacs* ("e-max").

Since there are several editor programs, you can choose one you're comfortable with. vi is probably the best choice because almost all Unix systems have it, but Emacs is also widely available. If you'll be doing simple editing only, Pico is a great choice. Although Pico is much less powerful than Emacs or vi, it's also a lot easier to learn. For this book, however, we'll focus on the rudiments of vi as it's the most widely available Unix editor, and there's a version of vi included with Mac OS X.

None of those editors has the same features as popular word-processing software within the graphical face of Mac OS X, but vi and Emacs are sophisticated, extremely flexible editors for all kinds of plain-text files: programs, email messages, and so on. Of course, you can opt to use an Aqua-based editor such as BBEdit or TextEdit with good results too, if you'd rather just sidestep editing while within the Terminal application. If you do, try using the open command within the Terminal to launch the editor with the proper file already loaded. For example: open -e myfile.txt.

By "plain text," we mean a file with only letters, numbers, and punctuation characters in it. Unix systems use plain-text files in many places: redirected input and output of Unix programs (Chapter 5), as shell setup files (see the section "Customizing Your Shell Environment" in Chapter 4), for shell scripts (shown in the section "Programming" in Chapter 10), for system configuration, and more. Text editors edit these files. When you use a word processor, though, although the screen may look as if the file is only plain text, the file probably also has hidden codes (nontext characters) in it. That's often true even if you tell the word processor to "Save as plain text." One easy way to check for nontext characters in a file is by reading the file with less; look for characters in reversed colors, codes such as <36>, and so on.

Fixing Those Pesky Carriage Returns

The only caveat regarding switching between Aqua applications and Unix applications for editing is that you might end up having to translate file formats along the way. Fortunately, this is easy with Unix.

One of the more awkward things about Apple putting a Mac graphical environment on top of a Unix core is that the two systems use different end-of-line character sequences. If you ever open up a file in an Aqua application and see lots of little boxes at the end of each line, or if you try to edit a file within Unix and find that it's littered with ^M sequences, you've hit the end-of-line problem.

To fix it, type in the following two commands at the shell (carefully):

```
% echo alias m2u tr '\015' '\012' >> ~/.cshrc
% echo alias u2m tr '\015' '\012' >> ~/.cshrc
```

Then type:

```
% source ~/.cshrc
```

Now, whenever you're working with Unix editing tools and you need to fix a Mac-format file, simply use m2u (Mac to Unix), as in:

```
% m2u < mac-format-file > unix-friendly-file
```

And if you find yourself in the opposite situation, where you're editing a Unix file in a Mac tool and it has some carriage-return weirdness, use the reverse (Unix to Mac) within Terminal before editing:

```
% u2m < unix-friendly-file > mac-format-file
```

Worthy of note is the helpful tr command, which makes it easy to translate all occurrences of one character to another. Use man tr to learn more about this powerful utility.

If you need to do word processing—making documents, envelopes, and so on—your best bet is to work with a program designed for that purpose such as Microsoft Office X or even TextEdit.

The vi Text Editor

The vi editor, originally written by Bill Joy at the University of California, Berkeley, is easy to use once you master the fundamental concept of a modal editor.

Modes can be best explained by thinking about your car stereo. When you have a tape in (or a CD), the "1" button does one task, but if you are listening to the radio, the very same button does something else (perhaps jump to pre-programmed station #1). The vi editor is exactly the same: in *command mode*, i jumps you into insert mode, but in *insert mode* it actually inserts an "i" into the text itself. The handiest key on your keyboard while you're learning vi is unquestionably ESC: if you're in insert mode, ESC will move you back into command mode, and if you're in command mode, it'll beep to let you know that all is well. Use ESC often, until you're completely comfortable keeping track of what mode you're in.

Start vi by typing its name; the argument is the filename you want to create or edit. For instance, to edit your *.cshrc* setup file, you would cd to your home directory and enter:

```
% vi .cshrc
```

The terminal fills with a copy of the file (and, because the file is short, some blank lines too, as denoted by the ~ at the beginning of the line), as shown in Figure 3-1.

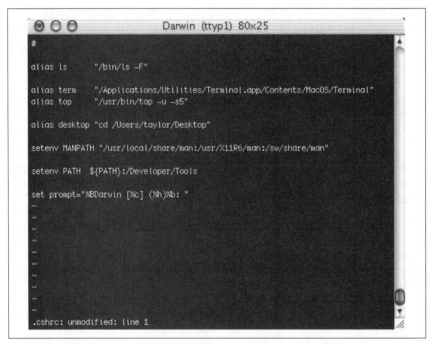

Figure 3-1. vi display while editing

The bottom row of the window is the status line, which indicates what file you're editing: *.cshrc: unmodified: line 1*. Quit the program by typing :q and pressing Return while in command mode.

vi tour

Let's take a tour through *vi*. In this example, you'll make a new file. You can call the file anything you want, but it's best to use only letters and numbers in the filename. For instance, to make a file named *sample*, enter the command vi sample. Let's start our tour now.

1. Your screen should look something like Figure 3-1, but the cursor should be on the top line and the rest of the lines should have the ~ blank line delimiter. Press i to move out of command mode and into insert mode, and you're ready to enter text.

2. Enter some lines of text. Make some lines too short (press Return before the line gets to the right margin). Make others too long; watch how vi wraps long lines. If you have another terminal window open with some text in it or an Aqua application, you can also use your mouse to copy text from another window and paste it into the vi window (always make sure you're in insert mode before you do this, however, or you could irrevocably mess up your file). To get a lot of text quickly, paste the same text more than once.

3. Let's practice moving around the file. To do this, we'll need to leave insert mode by pressing ESC once. Press it again and you'll hear a beep, reminding you that you are already in command mode. You can use your arrow keys to move around the file, but vi also lets you keep your fingers on the keyboard by using h j k l as the four motion keys (left, down, up, and right, respectively). vi works on all terminals, with or without a mouse, so it will probably ignore your mouse if you try to use it to move the cursor. If you've entered a lot of text, you can experiment with various movement commands use: H to jump to the first line on the screen, G to jump to the bottom of the file. You should also try the w and b commands, to move forward and backward by words. Also, 0 (zero) jumps to the beginning of the line, while $ jumps to the end.

   vi's search or "where is" command, */pattern*, can help you find a word quickly. It's handy even on a short file, where it can be quicker to type / and a word than to use the cursor-moving commands. The search command is also a good example of the way that vi can move your cursor to the status line so you can enter more information. Let's try it by typing /. You should see a display like Figure 3-2.

4. Notice that the cursor has jumped to the bottom of the display has changed since you started vi and is sitting next to a /. You can type a word or characters to search for, then press Return to do the search. After a search finishes, you can type n to repeat the search.

Figure 3-2. vi display while searching

5. If your text isn't in paragraphs separated by blank lines, break some of it into paragraphs. Put your cursor at the place you want to break the text and press i to move back into insert mode, then Return twice (once to break the line, another to make a blank line).

6. Now justify one paragraph. Put the cursor at the beginning of the paragraph and type !}fmt. Now the paragraph's lines should flow and fit neatly between the margins.

7. Text can be deleted by using x to delete the character that's under the cursor, or the powerful d command: dd deletes lines, dw deletes individual words, d$ deletes to the end of the line, d0 deletes to the beginning of the line, and dG deletes to the end of the file (if you're seeing a pattern and thinking that it's d + *motion specifier* you're absolutely correct). To undo the deletion, press u. You can also paste the deleted text with the p command.

8. The first step to copying text is to position your cursor. The copy command or "yank" works similar to the delete command. The yw command copies one word, yy yanks the line, y1 a single character, and ynw yanks *n* number words. Move the cursor to the line you want to copy and press yy. After repositioning your cursor to where you'd like the text copied, press p to paste the text.

9. As with any text editor, it's a good idea to save your work from vi every 5 or 10 minutes. That way, if something goes wrong on the computer or network, you'll be able to recover the edited buffer since the last time you saved it. When launching vi again, use the -r option with a *filename* to recover the edited buffer where the *filename* is the name of the file you were editing.

10. Try writing out your work with :w followed by Return. The bottom of the display will show the filename saved and the number of lines and characters in the file.

11. This part confuses some vi beginners. If you want to save the file with the same name it had when you started, just press :w and Return; that's all! You can also choose a different filename: type :w followed by the new filename. Press Return and it's saved.

12. Make one or two more small edits. Then, exit with :q. vi warns you that the file has not been saved. If you want to override the warning type :q!. You can also use a shortcut: :wq writes out your changes and quits vi.

That's it. There's a lot more you can learn about vi, and there's a considerably more sophisticated version of *vi* called *vim* that you can download for your Mac (*http://www.vim.org/*), if you want something even more powerful. In Table 3-1, you'll find a handy listing of some of the most common *vi* commands and their descriptions. O'Reilly has two very helpful books if you want to become a power user: *Learning the vi Editor* and *vi Editor Pocket Reference*.

Table 3-1. Common vi editing commands

Command	Meaning
/pattern	Search forward for specified pattern. Repeat search with n.
:q	Quit the edit session.
:q!	Quit, discarding any changes.
:w	Write (save) any changes out to the file.
:wq or ZZ	Write out any changes, then quit (shortcut).
a	Move into append mode (like insert mode, but you enter information after the cursor, not before).
b	Move backward one word.
w	Move forward one word.
d1G	Delete from the current point back to the beginning of the file.
dd	Delete the current line.
dG	Delete through end of file.
dw	Delete the following word.
ESC	Move into command mode.
h	Move backward one character.
l	Move forward one character.
i	Move into insert mode (ESC moves you back to command mode).
j	Move down one line.
k	Move up one line.
O	Open up a line above the current line and move into insert mode.
o	Open up a line below the current line and move into insert mode.

Managing Your Files

The tree structure of the Unix filesystem makes it easy to organize your files. After you make and edit some files, you may want to copy or move files from one directory to another, or rename files to distinguish different versions of a file. You may want to create new directories each time you start a different project. If you copy a file, it's worth learning about the subtle sophistication of the cp and CpMac commands: if you copy a file to a directory, it automatically reuses the filename in the new location. This can save lots of typing!

A directory tree can get cluttered with old files you don't need. If you don't need a file or a directory, delete it to free storage space on the disk. The following sections explain how to make and remove directories and files.

Creating Directories with mkdir

It's handy to group related files in the same directory. If you were writing a spy novel, you probably wouldn't want your intriguing files mixed with restaurant listings. You could create two directories: one for all the chapters in your novel (*spy*, for example), and another for restaurants (*boston.dine*).

To create a new directory, use the mkdir program. The syntax is:

    mkdir *dirname(s)*

dirname is the name of the new directory. To make several directories, put a space between each directory name. To continue our example, you would enter:

    % **mkdir spy boston.dine**

Copying Files

If you're about to edit a file, you may want to save a copy first. That makes it easy to get back the original version. You should use the cp program when copying plain files and directories. All other Macintosh files (that is, those with resource forks) should be copied with CpMac (available only if you have installed Apple's Mac OS X developer CD).

cp

The cp program can put a copy of a file into the same directory or into another directory. cp doesn't affect the original file, so it's a good way to keep an identical backup of a file.

To copy a file, use the command:

    cp *old new*

where *old* is a pathname to the original file and *new* is the pathname you want for the copy. For example, to copy the */etc/passwd* file into a file called *password* in your working directory, you would enter:

```
% cp /etc/passwd password
%
```

You can also use the form:

```
cp old olddir
```

This puts a copy of the original file *old* into an existing directory *olddir*. The copy will have the same filename as the original.

If there's already a file with the same name as the copy, cp replaces the old file with your new copy. This is handy when you want to replace an old copy with a newer version, but it can cause trouble if you accidentally overwrite a copy you wanted to keep. To be safe, use ls to list the directory before you make a copy there. Also, the Mac OS X version of cp has an -i (interactive) option that asks you before overwriting an existing file.

You can copy more than one file at a time to a single directory by listing the pathname of each file you want copied, with the destination directory at the end of the command line. You can use relative or absolute pathnames (see the section "The Unix Filesystem" in Chapter 2) as well as simple filenames. For example, let's say your working directory is */Users/carol* (from the filesystem diagram in Figure 2-1). To copy three files called *ch1*, *ch2*, and *ch3* from */Users/john* to a subdirectory called *work* (that's */Users/carol/work*), enter:

```
% cp ../john/ch1 ../john/ch2 ../john/ch3 work
```

Or, you could use wildcards and let the shell find all the appropriate files. This time, let's add the -i option for safety:

```
% cp -i ../john/ch[1-3] work
cp: overwrite work/ch2? n
```

There is already a file named *ch2* in the *work* directory. When cp asks, answer n to prevent copying *ch2*. Answering y would overwrite the old *ch2*.

As you saw in the section "Relative pathnames up" in Chapter 2, the shorthand form . puts the copy in the working directory, and .. puts it in the parent directory. For example, the following puts the copies into the working directory:

```
% cp ../john/ch[1-3] .
```

cp can also copy entire directory trees. Use the option -R, for "recursive." There are two arguments after the option: the pathname of the top-level directory you want to copy from and the pathname of the place where you want the top level of the copy to be. As an example, let's say that a new employee, Asha, has joined John and Carol. She needs a copy of John's *work* directory in her own home directory. See the filesystem diagram in Figure 2-1. Her home directory is */Users/asha*. If Asha's own *work* directory doesn't exist yet (important!), she could type the following commands:

```
% cd /Users
% cp -R john/work asha/work
```

Or, from her home directory, she could have typed cp -R ../john/work work. Either way, she'd now have a new subdirectory */Users/asha/work* with a copy of all files and subdirectories from */Users/john/work*.

 If you give cp -R the wrong pathnames, it can copy a directory tree into itself—running forever until your filesystem fills up!

If the copy seems to be taking a long time, stop cp with Control-Z, then explore the filesystem (ls -RF is handy for this). If all's okay, you can resume the copying by putting the cp job in the background (with bg) so it can finish its slow work. Otherwise, kill cp and do some cleanup—probably with rm -r, which we mention in the section "rmdir" later in this chapter. (Also, see the sections, "Running a Command in the Background" and "Canceling a Process" in Chapter 9.)

Problem checklist

The system says something like "cp: cannot copy file to itself."
> If the copy is in the same directory as the original, the filenames must be different.

The system says something like "cp: filename: no such file or directory."
> The system can't find the file you want to copy. Check for a typing mistake. If a file isn't in the working directory, be sure to use its pathname.

The system says something like "cp: permission denied."
> You may not have permission to copy a file created by someone else or copy it into a directory that does not belong to you. Use ls -l to find the owner and the permissions for the file, or ls -ld to check the directory. If you feel that you should be able to copy a file, ask the file's owner or a system staff person to change its access modes.

Copying Mac files with resources

The cp program works on plain files and directories, but the Macintosh system stores applications with resource information. These attributes used to be known as "resource forks," but in Mac OS X, file structures are more complex. For example, you'll recall the earlier invocation of the chess game:

```
% open /Applications/chess.app
```

A quick listing of the named folder *chess.app* is quite interesting. It's a directory with a folder *Contents*, and listing that reveals:

```
% ls /Applications/chess.app/Contents
Info.plist    MacOS/      PkgInfo      Resources/    version.plist
```

Because of the extra information required for each file, a special version of cp is used to copy Mac-format files. The program, CpMac, is included on the Developer CD-ROM that was included with your Mac OS X distribution. If you haven't installed the contents of this disk, you should. You can also download the disk image from the developer section of *http://developer.apple.com*.

CpMac is found in */Developer/Tools*. To copy the Chess application and its resources to your home directory invoke the following:

```
% /Developer/Tools/CpMac -r /Applications/chess.app ~
```

Of course, if you find yourself using MvMac or CpMac a lot, it'd save you lots of typing to either alias CpMac to */Developer/Tools/CpMac* or add */Developer/Tools* to your PATH. PATH is one of a set of environment variables that help the shell keep track of your particular session. Another variable you can see: ~ always expands to your home directory on the system (the directory you start out within when you launch a Terminal window). Information on customizing your path is found in the section, "Customizing Your Shell Environment" in Chapter 4.

Here's an example of how the resources are even hidden from ls:

```
% ls -al
-rw-r--r--  1 taylor  staff    408 Feb  4 23:41 Sample
-rw-r--r--  1 taylor  staff    324 Feb  4 23:07 a confusing name
-rw-r--r--  1 taylor  staff     64 Feb  4 23:07 another odd name
-rw-r--r--  1 taylor  staff      0 Feb  4 21:44 ch1.doc
-rw-r--r--  1 taylor  staff      0 Feb  4 21:44 ch2.doc
-rw-r--r--  1 taylor  staff      3 Feb  4 23:08 test:file
% ls -al */rsrc
-rw-r--r--  1 taylor  staff      0 Feb  4 23:41 Sample/rsrc
-rw-r--r--  1 taylor  staff      0 Feb  4 23:07 a confusing name/rsrc
-rw-r--r--  1 taylor  staff      0 Feb  4 23:07 another odd name/rsrc
-rw-r--r--  1 taylor  staff      0 Feb  4 21:44 ch1.doc/rsrc
-rw-r--r--  1 taylor  staff      0 Feb  4 21:44 ch2.doc/rsrc
-rw-r--r--  1 taylor  staff      0 Feb  4 23:08 test:file/rsrc
```

The resource files *rsrc* are there, but you can't see them with a regular ls command, which means that the regular cp command won't see them either.

As a simple rule of thumb, if using a regular cp command doesn't work, try CpMac instead. A good strategy is to try listing the */rscr* information too. If it's there, you'll want to pick it up on your copy for best results:

```
% ls Sample
Sample
```

```
% ls Sample/rsrc
Sample/rscr
% /Developer/Tools/CpMac Sample /Applications
%
```

Renaming and Moving Files with mv

To rename a file, use mv (move). The mv program can also move a file from one directory to another.

The mv command has the same syntax as the cp command:

```
mv old new
```

old is the old name of the file and *new* is the new name. mv will write over existing files, which is handy for updating old versions of a file. If you don't want to overwrite an old file, be sure that the new name is unique. The Mac OS X version of mv has an -i option for safety.

```
% mv chap1 intro
%
```

The previous example changed the file named *chap1* to *intro*. If you list your files with ls, you will see that the filename *chap1* has disappeared.

The mv command can also move a file from one directory to another. As with the cp command, if you want to keep the same filename, you only need to give mv the name of the destination directory.

There's also a MvMac command, analogous to the CpMac command explained earlier. Again, check by looking for a */rscr* resource file before copying (or after copying if you get unusual results when you view the file from the Finder) and use MvMac as needed.

Finding Files

If your account has lots of files, organizing them into subdirectories can help you find the files later. Sometimes you may not remember which subdirectory has a file. The find program can search for files in many ways; we'll look at two.

Change to your home directory so find will start its search there. Then carefully enter one of the following two find commands. (The syntax is strange and ugly—but find does the job!)

```
% cd
% find . -type f -name "chap*" -print
./chap2
./old/chap10b
% find . -type f -mtime -2 -print
./work/to_do
```

The first command looks in your working directory (.) and all its subdirectories for files (-type f) whose names start with *chap*. (find understands wildcards in filenames. Be sure to put quotes around any filename pattern with a wildcard in it, as we did in the example.) The second command looks for all files that have been created or modified in the last two days (-mtime -2). The relative pathnames that find finds start with a dot (./), the name of the working directory, which you can ignore. Worth noting is that -print displays the results on the screen, not on your printer.

Mac OS X has the 4.4 BSD Unix locate program. If it's been set up and maintained on your system, you can use locate to search part or all of a filesystem for a file with a certain name.* For instance, if you're looking for a file named *alpha-test*, *alphatest*, or something like that, try this:

```
% locate alpha
/Users/alan/alpha3
/usr/local/projects/mega/alphatest
```

You'll get the absolute pathnames of files and directories with *alpha* in their names. (If you get a lot of output, add a pipe to less. See the section "Piping to a Pager" in Chapter 6.) locate may or may not list protected, private files; its listings usually also aren't completely up to date. The fundamental difference between the two is that find lets you search by file type, contents, and much more, while locate is a simple list of all filenames on the system. To learn much more about find and locate, read your online documentation (see Chapter 10) or read the chapter about them in *Unix Power Tools* (O'Reilly).

Removing Files and Directories

You may have finished work on a file or directory and see no need to keep it, or the contents may be obsolete. Periodically removing unwanted files and directories frees storage space.

rm

The rm program removes files. Unlike moving an item to the trash, no opportunity exists to recover the item before you "empty the trash" when using rm.

The syntax is simple:

```
rm filename(s)
```

---

* By default, Mac OS X does support locate, but the script that updates the locate database is run only once a week, and your computer must be on and running for that to occur. If you want to update the database by hand, you can use sudo /usr/libexec/locate.updatedb if you have enabled sudo access administrative password.

rm removes the named files, as the following example shows:

```
% ls
chap10        chap2        chap5    cold
chap1a.old    chap3.old    chap6    haha
chap1b        chap4        chap7    oldjunk
% rm *.old chap10
% ls
chap1b    chap4    chap6    cold    oldjunk
chap2     chap5    chap7    haha
% rm c*
% ls
haha    oldjunk
%
```

When you use wildcards with rm, be sure you're deleting the right files! If you accidentally remove a file you need, you can't recover it unless you have a copy in another directory or in the system backups.

Do not enter rm * carelessly. It deletes all the files in your working directory.

Here's another easy mistake to make: you want to enter a command such as rm c* (remove all filenames starting with "c") but instead enter rm c * (remove the file named c and all files!).

It's good practice to list the files with ls before you remove them. Or, if you use rm's -i (interactive) option, rm asks you whether you want to remove each file.

rmdir

Just as you can create new directories, you can remove them with the rmdir program. As a precaution, rmdir won't let you delete directories that contain any files or subdirectories; the directory must first be empty. (The rm -r command removes a directory and everything in it. It can be dangerous for beginners, though.)

The syntax is:

```
rmdir dirname(s)
```

If a directory you try to remove does contain files, you get a message like "rmdir: *dirname* not empty."

To delete a directory that contains some files:

1. Enter cd *dirname* to get into the directory you want to delete.
2. Enter rm * to remove all files in that directory.
3. Enter cd .. to go to the parent directory.
4. Enter rmdir *dirname* to remove the unwanted directory.

Problem checklist

I still get the message "dirname not empty" even after I've deleted all the files.

Use `ls -a` to check that there are no hidden files (names that start with a period) other than . and .. (the working directory and its parent). The following command is good for cleaning up hidden files (which aren't matched by a simple wildcard such as *):

```
% rm .[a-zA-Z]* .??*
```

Files on Other Operating Systems

Chapter 7 includes the section, "Transferring Files," which explains ways to transfer files across a network—possibly to non-Unix operating systems. Mac OS X has the capability of connecting to a variety of different filesystems remotely, including Microsoft Windows, other Unix systems, and even Web-based filesystems.

If the Windows-format filesystem is *mounted* with your other filesystems, you'll be able to use its files by typing a Unix-like pathname. For instance, from our Mac, we can access the Windows file *C:\WORD\REPORT.DOC* through the pathname */Volumes/winc/word/report.doc*. Indeed, most external volumes are automatically mounted within the */Volumes* directory.

CHAPTER 4

Customizing Your Session

One of the great pleasures of using Unix with Mac OS X surrounding it is that you get the benefit of a truly wonderful graphical application environment and the underlying power of the raw Unix interface. A match made in heaven!

This chapter discusses how to customize your Terminal environment both from the graphical user interface using Terminal → Preferences and from the Unix shell by using shell configuration files.

Launching Terminal

Launch Terminal and you have a dull, uninspiring white window with black text that says 'Welcome to Darwin!" and a shell prompt. But that's okay. We can fix it.

Changing Terminal Preferences

To change the display preferences in the Terminal application, go to the Terminal menu and choose Preferences.... You see a display similar to Figure 4-1.

Along the window's top, notice that a number of different preferences are configurable: Startup, Shell, Window, Text & Colors, Buffer, Emulation, and Activity. The icons suggest what each does, but let's have a closer look anyway, particularly since some of these settings definitely *should* be changed in our view. It's worth pointing out that these changes affect *new windows* not the current window.

Startup Preferences

When you first open Terminal Preferences, the Startup Preferences are displayed, as shown in Figure 4-1. The default behavior is to launch a new

Figure 4-1. Startup Preferences

blank shell window each time the program is started, so you're ready to start typing commands immediately. Unless you're an advanced user, don't change this behavior. Instead, let's look at what's on the other preference screens, which you can view by clicking on each icon at the top of the Preferences window.

Shell Preferences

As Figure 4-2 reveals, there are a number of behavioral choices you can make on this panel, including whether you want each window to have its own login shell associated with your account, or whether all Terminal windows should run a specified shell (in this case, */bin/tcsh*). In Mac OS X you're probably the only person who uses your computer, so if your login shell is acceptable to you, leaving the shell setting to reference the login shell is your best bet.

Also on this panel you can specify that when a login shell exits, the Terminal application can close the window, close the window only if the shell exited cleanly (that is, returned a nonzero status code, which means that all the applications gracefully shut down), or never close the window. If you like to study what you've done and want to be forced to explicitly close the Terminal window, the last choice is for you. Otherwise, either of the first two will work fine.

Finally, you can specify a nonstandard string encoding if you're working with an unusual language or font. By default, the UTF-8 (Unicode 8-bit) encoding is quite acceptable and will also keep you out of trouble with more complex character sets that Unix might not understand correctly.

Figure 4-2. Shell Preferences

Window Preferences

If you have a large display, or are running at a higher resolution than 800x600, you'll find it quite helpful to enlarge the Terminal window to offer a bigger space within which to work. Our default is 80 characters wide by 40 lines tall, as shown in Figure 4-3.

The title of each Terminal window can be fine tuned too: you might find the device name (what you'd get if you typed tty at the shell prompt) and the window size particularly helpful.

If you want to change the Terminal window title at any point, you can use the Set Title option by either choosing it from the Shell menu or typing ⌘-Shift-T. The resulting Terminal Inspector window, as shown in Figure 4-4, lets you fine tune the appearance of an existing window (by contrast, the preferences only affect future windows, not those that are already open).

Text & Colors Preferences

The area that you'll probably fine tune more than any other is Text & Colors. Here you can specify a different (or larger) font, and change the foreground, background, bold, cursor, and selection colors, as well as define the shape of your cursor within the Terminal window. The default is black text

Figure 4-3. Window Preferences

Figure 4-4. Terminal Inspector window

on a white background, but we find that light text on a dark background is easier to read for extended periods. One suggested preference is where the background is a very dark blue, the cursor is yellow, normal text is light yellow, bold text is light green, and the selection is a dark green.

While you can choose any font available on your system, you'll find that your display is much more comprehensible if you stick to monospace or fixed-width type. Monaco is a very good choice, and is the default typeface for the Terminal application.

Buffer Preferences

The settings in this area probably don't need changing. The scrollback buffer allows you to scroll back and review earlier commands and command output. The default value of 10,000 lines should be more than enough for most people. If you want to use less memory, you can put in a smaller number or completely disable the scrollback buffer, rather than specifying a size.

You can also choose whether the Terminal should wrap long lines (not all Unix programs will wrap long lines, and so they might disappear off the edge of the window if this option isn't set), or whether you should automatically jump to the bottom of the scroll buffer upon input, if you've scrolled back to examine something that transpired earlier in your session. These options are set by default, and you should probably leave them that way.

Emulation Preferences

These preferences don't need to be altered by most users. If you're using the Emacs text editor, however, you will want to select "Option (alt) key acts as meta key" to allow meta-key sequences. What's a meta-key sequence? Emacs uses lots of Control, Alt, Control-Alt, and similar key sequences for complex commands, and one modifier it uses is a new-to-Mac-users "meta" key. If you use Emacs, you'll see when the meta key is necessary.

 Some Titanium PowerBook G4s have an inordinate delay before emitting audio, and if you've got one of these and you've noticed it as a problem, select "Mute terminal bell" to neatly sidestep the problem. This also has the nice side effect of preventing people around you knowing when you've made a mistake too, of course.

Otherwise, it's best to leave "translate newlines to carriage returns" so that you can ignore the difference in end-of-line sequences in Mac files versus Unix files, and to avoid strict "vt100" emulation, because it can get in the way of some of the newer Mac OS X Unix utilities. Whether or not you enable Option-Click for positioning the cursor might depend on whether you're a Unix purist (for whom the "good old keyboard" works fine) or whether you're trying to simplify things. Beware that if you do enable

Option-Click positioning, it won't work in all cases, only when you're in a full-screen application such as Emacs.

Activity monitor

One of the more subtle capabilities of the Terminal application is that it can keep track of what applications you're running so it can be smart about confirming window close requests: if there's something still running in the window, it'll pop up a dialog box asking if you're sure you want to quit. This feature is very helpful if you are prone to accidentally click the wrong window element or push the wrong key sequence. We recommend you enable the activity monitor to help avoid accidentally closing windows (and automatically killing all the processes running within those windows).

Customizing Your Shell Environment

The Unix shell reads a number of configuration files when it starts up. These configuration files are really *shell programs*, so they are extraordinarily powerful. Shell programming is beyond the scope of this book. For more detail, see Paul DuBois' book, *Using csh and tcsh* (O'Reilly). Because Unix is a multiuser system, there are two possible locations for the configuration files: one applies to all users of the system and another to each individual user.

The system-wide setup files that are read by *tcsh*, the default shell for Mac OS X, are found in */usr/share/init/tcsh*. You only have permission to change these system-wide files if you are logged in as root. However, you can create an additional file called *.tcshrc* in your home directory that will add additional commands to be executed whenever you start a new Terminal window. (If you configure Terminal to use another shell, such as the Bourne shell, the C shell, or the Z shell, you'll need to set up different configuration files, which we don't discuss.) The system-wide setup files are read first, then the user-specific ones, so commands in your *.tcshrc* file may override those in the system-wide files.

The *.tcshrc* file can contain any shell command that you want to run automatically whenever you create a new Terminal. Some typical examples include changing the shell prompt, setting environment variables (values that control the operation of other Unix utilities), setting aliases, or adding to the search path (where the shell searches for programs to be run). A *.tcshrc* file could look like this:

```
set prompt="%/ %h% "
setenv LESS 'eMq'
alias desktop "cd /Users/taylor/Desktop"
date
```

This sample *.tcshrc* file issues the following commands:

- The line with set prompt tells the shell to use a different prompt than the standard one. We'll explain the details of prompt setting in the section "Changing Your Prompt" later in this chapter.

- The line with setenv LESS tells the less program which options you want to set every time you use it. Not all commands recognize environment variables, but for those that do, this saves you the trouble of typing the options on every less command line. Environment variables have many uses within Unix. A good place to learn more about them is the book *Unix Power Tools*, by Jerry Peek, Tim O'Reilly, and Mike Loukides (O'Reilly).

- The line that begins with alias defines a new, custom command that your shell will recognize just as if it were a built-in Unix command. Aliases are a great way to save shorthand names for long, complicated Unix command lines, or even to fix common mistakes you might make when typing command lines. This particular alias creates a command for going right to the Desktop directory. We give a brief tutorial on creating aliases later in this chapter.

- The date line simply runs the date command to print the time and date when you open a new Terminal window. You probably don't want to do this, but we want you to understand that you can put in any command that you could type at the shell prompt, and have it automatically executed whenever a new shell starts up.

By default, the *.tcshrc* file doesn't exist in your home directory. Only the system-wide configuration files are read. But if you create the file, it will be read and its contents executed the next time you start a shell. (You can also create a file called *.logout* to contain commands to be executed when you end a shell.) You can create or change these files with a text editor, such as vi (see "The vi Text Editor" in Chapter 3). Don't use a word processor that breaks long lines or puts special nontext codes into the file. Any changes you make to these files will take effect the next time you log in (or, in some cases, when you start a new shell—such as opening a new Terminal window). Unfortunately, it's not always easy to know which shell setup file you should change.* And an editing mistake in your shell setup file can keep you from logging in to your account! We suggest that beginners get help from

---

* In addition to *.tcshrc*, the shell will also read and execute files called *.login*, *.cshrc*, and *.logout*. Some files are read by login shells and others by non-login shells. Some are read by subshells, others aren't. Some terminal windows open login shells, others don't. And if you're using the Bourne shell, still other files, such as *.profile*, are read instead. We focus only on *.tcshrc* here, but a more advanced Unix book can provide more information once you need it.

experienced users, and don't make changes to these files at all if you're about to do some critical work with your account, unless there's some reason you have to make the changes immediately.

You can execute any customization command we show you here from the command line as well. In this case, the changes are in effect only until you close that window or quit Terminal.

For example, to change the default options for less so it will clear the Terminal window before it shows each new page of text, you could add the -c option to the LESS environment variable. The command would look something like this:

```
% setenv LESS 'eMqc'
```

(If you don't want some of the less options we've shown, you could leave those letters out.) Unix has many other configuration commands to learn about; the sources listed in Chapter 10 can help.

Just as you can execute the setup commands from the command line, the converse is true: any command that you can execute from the command line can be executed automatically when you log in by placing it in your setup file. (Running interactive commands such as vi or ftp from your setup file isn't a good idea, though.)

Changing Your Prompt

The easiest customization you can perform is to change your prompt. By default, *tcsh* on Darwin has a shell prompt made up of your computer hostname, your account name, and a percent sign (for example: [dsl-132:~] taylor%). If you'd rather have something else, it's time to edit your own *.tcshrc* file. Use the vi editor (you might need to flip back to "The vi Text Editor" in Chapter 3) to create a file called *.tcshrc* in your home directory (*/Users/yourname*) and add the following to the end of the file: set prompt="% ". You can also change the prompt for a single session by invoking the command as follows:

```
[dsl-132:~]taylor% set prompt="% "
%
```

This command will give you a simple, spare % prompt with nothing else. (The % is traditional for shells derived from the Berkeley Unix C Shell, while $ is traditional for shells derived from the original Bell Labs Bourne Shell.) It's not necessary—you could use a colon, a greater than sign, or any other prompt character—but it is a nice convention, because it will immediately tell an advanced user what kind of shell you are using.

If that's all you could do to set your prompt, it wouldn't be very interesting, though. There are a number of special character sequences that, when used to define the prompt, cause the shell to print out various bits of useful data. Table 4-1 shows a partial list of these special character sequences for fine tuning your prompt.

Table 4-1. Favorite percent escape sequences for tcsh prompts

Value	Meaning
%/	The current working directory
%~	The current working directory, with your home represented as ~ and other users homes represented as ~user
%c	The trailing element of the current working directory, with ~ substitution
%h	The current command history number
%M	The full hostname
%m	The hostname up to the first dot
%B/%b	Start/Stop bold mode (matches the bold color in the Terminal color preferences)
%t	Time of day in 12-hour (a.m./p.m.) format
%T	Time of day in 24-hour format
%n	The username

Experiment and see what you can create that will meet your needs and be fun too. For many years, a popular Unix prompt was:

```
% set prompt="Yes, Master? "
```

It might be a bit obsequious, but on the other hand, how many people in your life call you "Master"?

One prompt sequence that we like is:

```
% set prompt="%/ %h% "
```

This prompt sequence shows the current working directory, followed by a space, and the current history number, and then a percent sign to remind the user that this is *csh* or *tcsh*. For example, the prompt might read:

```
/Users/taylor 55%
```

This tells me immediately that */Users/taylor* is my current directory, and that I'm on the 55th command I've executed. (Because you can use the arrow keys to scroll back to previous commands, as described in the section, "Recalling Previous Commands" in Chapter 1, this is no longer as important, but there is a very powerful command history syntax built into *tcsh* that allows you to recall a previous command by number. If you're familiar with this syntax, making the command history number part of the prompt can be handy.) On multiuser systems, it's not a bad idea to put the user-name into the prompt as well, so you always know who the system thinks you are.

Creating Aliases

The flexibility of Unix is simultaneously its greatest strength and downfall; the operating system can do just about anything you can imagine (the command-line interface is certainly far more flexible than Aqua, the graphical interface!) but it's very difficult to remember every single flag to every command. That's where shell aliases can be a real boon. A shell alias is a simple mechanism that lets you create your own command names that act exactly as you desire.

For example, we really like the -a flag to be included every time we list a directory with ls, so we created an alias:

```
% alias ls      "/bin/ls -a"
```

This indicates that each time we type ls in the shell, the /bin/ls command is going to be run, and it's going to automatically have the -a flag specified. To have this available in your next session, make sure you remember to add the alias to your *.cshrc* file too.

You can also have aliases that let you jump quickly to common locations, a particularly helpful trick when in Mac OS X:

```
% alias desktop "cd /Users/taylor/Desktop"
```

There are many aliases predefined in the *tcsh* shell. You can list active aliases all by typing alias without any arguments:

```
% alias
.         pwd
..        cd ..
cd..      cd ..
cdwd      cd `pwd`
cwd       echo $cwd
desktop   cd /Users/taylor/Desktop
ff        find . -name !:1 -print
files     find !:1 -type f -print
l         ls -lg
line      sed -n '!:1 p' !:2
list_all_hostnames      grep -v "^#" /etc/hosts
ll        ls -lag !* | more
ls        /bin/ls -F
pp        winname prosperpoint;ssh -l taylor prosperpoint.com;winname Darwin
staging   winname staging;ssh -l taylor staging.intuitive.com;winname Darwin
term      /Applications/Utilities/Terminal.app/Contents/MacOS/Terminal
winname   echo -n '^[]0;!^^G'
word      grep !* /usr/share/dict/web2
```

Have an alias you really want to omit? You can use unalias for that. For example, unalias ls would remove the -a flag addition. Drop the unalias command into your *.cshrc* file and it'll ensure that the system alias won't bother you ever again.

Further Customization

There's not much more you can do with the Terminal application than what's shown in this chapter, but there's an infinite amount of customization possible with the *tcsh* shell (or any other shell you might have picked). To learn more about how to customize your shell, read the manpage. Be warned, though, the *tcsh* manpage is over 5,800 lines long!

Oh, and in case you're wondering, manpages are the Unix version of online help documentation. Just about every command-line (Unix) command has a corresponding manpage with lots of information on starting flags, behaviors, and much more. You can access any manpage by simply typing man *cmd*. Start with man man to learn more about the man system.

For more information on customizing *tcsh*, see Paul DuBois' book, *Using csh and tcsh*, or *Unix Power Tools, Second Edition*, by Jerry Peek, Tim O'Reilly, and Mike Loukides, both available from O'Reilly.

## CHAPTER 5

Printing

Working in the Macintosh environment, you're used to a simple and elegant printer interface, particularly in OS X, where Print Center makes it a breeze to add new printers and configure your existing printers. The Unix environment has never had a printing interface that even comes close in usability, and while the standard print command in Unix is lpr, getting it to work on OS X involves reconfiguring your system and a number of tricky system administration tasks best avoided if you're not a Unix expert.

 If you do want to try, see Configuring Your Printer at the end of this chapter for some suggestions on how to proceed.

Formatting and Print Commands

The good news is that Apple has included a couple of alternative command-line interfaces to printers, notably atprint for AppleTalk–based printers, and Print, a program that's supposed to inject your print jobs into the regular Aqua print queue.

Regardless of what program you're going to use for printing, before you print a file on a Unix system, you may want to reformat it to adjust the margins, highlight some words, and so on. Most files can also be printed without reformatting, but the raw printout might not look quite as nice. Further, some printers accept only PostScript, which means you'll need to use a text-to-PostScript filter such as enscript for good results. Before we cover printing itself, let's look at both pr and enscript to see how they work.

pr

The pr program does minor formatting of files on the terminal screen or for a printer. For example, if you have a long list of names in a file, you can format it onscreen into two or more columns.

The syntax is:

```
pr option(s) filename(s)
```

pr changes the format of the file only on the screen or on the printed copy; it doesn't modify the original file. Table 5-1 lists some pr options.

Table 5-1. Some pr options

Option	Description
-k	Produces k columns of output
-d	Double-spaces the output (may not work on all versions of pr)
-h header	Takes the next item as a report header
-t	Eliminates printing of header and top/bottom margins

Other options allow you to specify the width of columns, set the page length, etc. For a complete list of options, see the manpage, man pr.

Before using pr, here are the contents of a sample file named *food*:

```
% cat food
Sweet Tooth
Bangkok Wok
Mandalay
Afghani Cuisine
Isle of Java
Big Apple Deli
Sushi and Sashimi
Tio Pepe's Peppers
%
```

Let's use pr options to make a two-column report with the header Restaurants:

```
% pr -2 -h "Restaurants" food

Feb  4  9:58 2002  Restaurants    Page 1

Sweet Tooth              Isle of Java
Bangkok Wok              Big Apple Deli
Mandalay                 Sushi and Sashimi
Afghani Cuisine          Tio Pepe's Peppers
.
.
.
%
```

The text is output in two-column pages. The top of each page has the date and time, header (or name of the file, if header is not supplied), and page number. To send this output to the printer instead of the terminal screen, create a pipe to the printer program—usually atprint or lpr. See the section "Pipes and Filters" in Chapter 6 for more information.

enscript

One reason for the success of the Macintosh has been its integrated support of PostScript for printing. Allowing sophisticated imaging and high-quality text, PostScript printers are quite the norm in the Mac world. However, this proves a bit of a problem from the Unix perspective, because Unix commands are used to working with regular text without any special PostScript formatting included.

Translating plain text into PostScript is the job of enscript. The enscript program has a remarkable number of different command flags, allowing you access to all the layout and configuration options you're familiar with from the Page Setup and Print dialog boxes in Aqua.

The most helpful command flags are summarized in Table 5-2 (you can learn about all the many options to enscript by reading the enscript manpage). A typical usage is enscript -p- Sample.txt | atprint to send the file to a printer or enscript -psample.ps sample.txt to output to the file *sample.ps*.

Table 5-2. Useful enscript options

Option	Description
-B	Do not print page headers.
-f *font*	Print body text using *font* (the default is Courier10).
-j	Print borders around columns (you can turn on multicolumn output with -1 or -2).
-p *file*	Send output to *file*. Use - to stream output to standard out (for pipes).
-r	Rotate printout 90 degrees, printing in landscape mode instead of portrait (the default).
-W *lang*	Output in the specified language. Default is PostScript, but enscript also supports HTML, overstrike, and RTF.

atprint

The standard way to print within the Unix environment is to use either lp or lpr (Mac OS X has lpr) but it's quite difficult to configure properly on Mac OS X. Instead, if you have an AppleTalk printer, you'll be relieved to know that there are a set of easy-to-use AppleTalk-aware Unix commands included with Mac OS X. The most important of the commands is atprint, which lets you easily stream any Unix output to a printer.

To start working with the AppleTalk tools, run atlookup, which lists all the AppleTalk devices recognized on the network (and that can be quite a few):

```
% atlookup
Found 4 entries in zone *
ff1d.a0.80        Dave Taylor's Computer:Darwin
ff01.04.08        PET:SNMP Agent
ff01.04.9d        PET:LaserWriter
ff01.04.9e        PET:LaserJet 2100
```

You can see that the PET printer (an HP LaserJet2100) appears with two different AppleTalk addresses. Fortunately, that can safely be ignored as well as the other AppleTalk devices that show up in the list. The important thing is that the atlookup command confirmed that there is indeed an AppleTalk printer online.

To select a specific AppleTalk printer as the default printer for the atprint command, run the oddly named at_cho_prn command. The trick is that you need to run this command as *root* or administrator. If you enabled sudo you can use it to easily run the program as *root*:

```
% sudo at_cho_prn
Password:
  1: ff01.04.9dtPET:LaserWriter

ITEM number (0 to make no selection)?1
Default printer is:PET:LaserWriter@*
status: idle
```

Now, finally, the PET printer is selected as the default AppleTalk printer, and all subsequent invocations of atprint will be sent to that printer without having to remember its exact name.

What if you don't know your administrative password? Be careful when resetting your administrative password. If you forgot your password, read the Mac OS Help to direct you. You might need to reboot your computer off your original OS X install CD-ROM, then when you get to the installer, select the Set Administrative Password... option from the File menu. The program will then prompt you for a new password and set it for your machine. Reboot again (without the CD-ROM), and you should be set forever.

Because most of the printers available through AppleTalk on a Macintosh network are PostScript printers, it's essential to use the enscript program to ensure the output is in proper PostScript format. As an example, the following prints the intro manpage (an introduction to the manpage system) on the PET printer, properly translated into PostScript:

```
% man intro | enscript -p- | atprint
man: Formatting manual page...
Looking for PET:LaserWriter@*.
```

```
Trying to connect to PET:LaserWriter@*.
[ 1 pages * 1 copy ] left in -
atprint: printing on PET:LaserWriter@*.
```

Pipes (command sequences with | between the commands) are covered in more detail in Chapter 6.

lpr

The other possibility for printing is the standard Unix command lpr for sending files to a printer. The syntax is:

```
lpr option(s) filename(s)
```

After you enter the command to print a file, the shell prompt returns to the screen and you can enter another command. However, seeing the prompt doesn't mean your file has been printed. Your file has been added to the printer queue to be printed in turn.

Your system administrator has hopefully set up a default printer on your system. If not, you might want to use atprint if you have an AppleTalk printer, or simply open your files in an Aqua application such as TextEdit and print from there. If you really want to use lpr and it isn't configured, see the section "Configuring Your LPR Printer" later in this chapter for some suggestions on getting it to work on your Macintosh.

To print a file named *bills* on the default printer, use the lpr command, as in this example:

```
% lpr -Plj bills
%
```

lpr has no output if everything was accepted and queued properly. If you need ID numbers for lpr jobs, use the lpq program to view the print queue (see the section "lpq" later in this chapter). The file *bills* will be sent to a printer called *lj*. lpr has several options. Table 5-3 lists three of them.

Table 5-3. Some lpr options

Command	Description
-P*printer*	Use given *printer* name if there is more than one printer at your site. The printer names are assigned by the system administrator.
-#	Print # copies of the file.
-m	Notify sender by email when printing is done.

Windowing applications such as Microsoft Office use a completely different print queuing system that's part of the Aqua environment. Those jobs won't show up in the Darwin print queue, even if they're going to the same printer.

Problem checklist

lpr returns "jobs queued, but cannot start daemon."

Your system is probably not configured properly for an lpr printer. If you have a named lpr printer that works, try the command again with the P*printername* option. If not, you might want to try using atprint or opening up your files in TextEdit and printing from the Aqua environment.

My printout hasn't come out.

See whether the printer is printing now. If it is, other users may have made requests to the same printer ahead of you, and your file should be printed in turn. The following section explains how to check the print requests.

If no file is printing, check the printer's paper supply, physical connections, and power switch. The printer may also be hung (stalled). If it is, ask other users or system staff people for advice.

My printout is garbled or doesn't look anything like the file did on my terminal.

The printer may not be configured to handle the kind of file you're printing. For instance, a file in plain-text format will look fine when previewed in your Terminal window, but look like gibberish when you try to print it. If the printer understands only PostScript, make sure that you use enscript to translate the plain-text format into acceptable PostScript.

Viewing the Printer Queue

If you want to find out how many files or "requests" for output are ahead of yours in the printer queue, use the program named lpq. The lprm command lets you cancel print jobs from the lpr queue.

Remember that if you want to check on the status of a print job from an Aqua application such as Internet Explorer or even Terminal, you'll want to go into Applications → Utilities → Print Center. Then double-click on the printer to see the state of the queue.

lpq

The lpq command shows what's currently printing and what's in the queue:

```
% lpq -Plj
waiting for 198.76.82.151  to come up
Rank    Owner    Job  Files                         Total Size
1st     root     8    (standard input)              12244 bytes
2nd     taylor   9    (standard input)              13018 bytes
%
```

The first line displays the printer status. If the printer is disabled or out of paper, you may see different messages on this first line. Here you can see

---

that the queue system is waiting for the printer to "come up" (it's turned off). Jobs are printed in the order indicated in the lpq output. The Job number is important, because you can remove print jobs from the queue (if you're the owner) with lprm.

lprm

lprm terminates lpr requests. You can specify either the ID of the request (displayed by lpq) or the name of the printer.

If you don't have the request ID, get it from lpq, then use lprm. Specifying the request ID cancels the request, even if it is currently printing:

```
% lprm -Plj 8
dfA008dsl-132.dsldesigns.com dequeued
cfA008dsl-132.dsldesigns.com dequeued
```

To cancel whatever request is currently printing, regardless of its ID, simply enter lprm and the printer name:

```
% lprm -Plj
dfA009dsl-132.dsldesigns.com dequeued
cfA009dsl-132.dsldesigns.com dequeued
```

lprm tells you the actual filenames removed from the printer queue (which you probably don't need).

Configuring Your LPR Printer

While there are a great many areas of Mac OS X that are enhanced by the addition of Unix as the low-level operating system, one area has become more complex: printing. If you only live in the world of Aqua, it's not too bad because Print Center manages all your needs, but if you want to print from the Unix command line and you don't have an AppleTalk printer, you've got a bit of a tinkering job ahead of you.

If you do have a printer accessible through AppleTalk, flip back a few pages and read the section about the atprint command, or use man atprint to learn how to simplify your life considerably.

Otherwise, configuring your printer requires four steps: adding an entry to */etc/printcap* for the printer, creating a spool directory and log file skeleton, importing the *printcap* entry into NetInfo, and adding the printer to Print Center.

To do this, you'll need both your Unix root password and your system administrator password. If you're unsure about your Unix root password, you can go into NetInfo and search the help system.

Editing /etc/printcap

The first step is to edit the printer capabilities database *letc/printcap*. You need to be root to do this, so it's easiest to use the sudo command to simply run the edit command as root:

```
% sudo vi /etc/printcap
```

This file contains lots of cryptic information that is attempting to define the capabilities and interface for each known printer accessible from Unix. The default entry in the file is for a local printer that's accessible through the */dev/lp* device:

```
lp|local line printer:\
    :lp=/dev/lp:sd=/var/spool/output/lpd:lf=/var/log/lpd-errs:
```

Odds are that this printer configuration is not going to work for you, however, so comment it out and add a new one for the new printer. In this example, 198.76.82.151 is the IP address of an HP LaserJet 2100TN Ethernet printer, which we'll call *lj* for the Unix system. If your printer has a unique hostname, that's better to use than the IP address, but either way, carefully duplicate the following:

```
lj:\
    :lp=:rm=198.76.82.151:rp=lp:sd=/var/spool/lpd/lj:lf=/var/log/lj-errs.log:
```

The only lines in the file that should be uncommented (that is, that don't have # as their first character) are those two above. Save the file and exit.

Creating the Spool Directory and Log File

The spool directory and log file specified in the new *printcap* entry must now be created and have their permissions set appropriately. Again, you'll need to be root or you can use the sudo shortcut for each line. For simplicity, switch to root (notice the command prompt changes to a #) for these commands:

```
% su root
Password:
#
```

The spool directory */usr/spool/lpd* should already exist on your system, so we need to create the specific subdirectory that matches the spool directory name listed in the *printcap* entry:

```
# cd /var/spool/lpd
# mkdir lj ; chown root.daemon lj
```

Then a *.seq* file should be created so the system can keep track of print job sequence numbers:

```
# cd lj
# touch .seq ; chown root.daemon .seq
```

Finally, create the empty log file and set the appropriate permissions:

```
# cd /var/log
# touch lj-errs ; chown root.daemon lj-errs ; chmod 644 lj-errs
```

Loading the printcap Entry into NetInfo

One innovation that Apple has added to Unix as part of Mac OS X is the centralized NetInfo database. We've bumped into it when looking at */etc/passwd* (since user accounts are stored in NetInfo now, not */etc/passwd* as on other Unix systems). NetInfo also manages printers on the Unix system, and so it's necessary to inform it about the new printer that's just been added.

Fortunately, the command-line utility niload knows how to read the *printcap* file, so it's a single step:

```
# niload printcap / < /etc/printcap
```

Enter that command carefully: note that there's a space after printcap and before /.

Now you can launch NetInfo and ensure that the printer was configured properly. Go into Applications → Utilities → NetInfo Manager. Upon launch, it shows a multi-pane window, much of which is beyond the scope of this book.

To verify that your new printer was added, click on "printers" in the middle column, then your new printer should be in the right pane. Click on that and you should see the bottom pane display information very similar to Figure 5-1.

If all looks similar, you can quit NetInfo and proceed to the next step. If things are different, or there's no printer shown, go back and ensure that you entered the niload command exactly as shown earlier.

Adding the Printer to Print Center

The final step in this process is to launch Print Center (Applications → Utilities) and click on the Add Printer... button. Ensure that you're selecting from the Directory Services printers, and you should see the new printer appear, just as in Figure 5-2.

Select the printer, click Add, and you should be good to go.

To try printing, go back to the Terminal application and feed a PostScript file to the new printer:

```
# lpr -Plj MySample.ps
# lpq
#
```

Make sure you exit as *root*.

Figure 5-1. Verifying an LPR printer in NetInfo Manager

Figure 5-2. Adding the NetInfo printer to Print Center

Important Caveat

Configuring LPR printers in Unix is more of a voodoo art than a science, so if you can't get this to work, your best bet is to explore some of the Mac OS X Unix support and discussion groups and also to check in with the Apple Knowledge Base. See Chapter 10 for the web addresses.

CHAPTER 6

Redirecting I/O

Many Unix programs read input (such as a file) and write output. In this chapter, we discuss Unix programs that handle their input and output in a standard way. This lets them work with each other.

This chapter generally *doesn't* apply to full-screen programs, such as the Pico editor, that take control of your whole Terminal window. (The pager programs, less, and more do work together in this way.) It also doesn't apply to graphical programs, such as the Finder or Internet Explorer, that open their own windows on your screen.

Standard Input and Standard Output

What happens if you don't give a filename argument on a command line? Most programs will take their input from your keyboard instead (after you press Return to start the program running, that is). Your Terminal keyboard is the program's *standard input*.

As a program runs, the results are usually displayed on your Terminal screen. The Terminal screen is the program's *standard output*. So, by default, each of these programs takes its information from the standard input and sends the results to the standard output. These two default cases of input/output (I/O) can be varied. This is called *I/O redirection*.

If a program doesn't normally read from files, but reads from its standard input, you can give a filename by using the < (less-than symbol) operator. For example, the mail program (see the section "Sending Mail from a Shell Prompt" in Chapter 8) normally reads the message to send from your keyboard. Here's how to use the input redirection operator to count the number of lines in the file *to_do* :

```
% wc -l < to_do
%
```

If a program writes to its standard output, which is normally the screen, you can make it write to a file instead by using the greater-than symbol (>) operator. The pipe operator (|) sends the standard output of one program to the standard input of another program. Input/output redirection is one of the most powerful and flexible Unix features.

Putting Text in a File

Instead of always letting a program's output come to the screen, you can redirect output to a file. This is useful when you'd like to save program output, or when you put files together to make a bigger file.

cat

cat, which is short for "concatenate," reads files and outputs their contents one after another, without stopping.

To display files on the standard output (your screen), use:

    cat *file(s)*

For example, let's display the contents of the file */etc/passwd*. This system file describes users' accounts. (Mac OS X has a more complete list in the NetInfo database.)

```
% cat /etc/passwd
nobody:*:-2:-2:Unprivileged User:/dev/null:/dev/null
root:*:0:0:System Administrator:/var/root:/bin/tcsh
daemon:*:1:1:System Services:/var/root:/dev/null
unknown:*:99:99:Unknown User:/dev/null:/dev/null
www:*:70:70:World Wide Web Server:/Library/WebServer:/dev/null
%
```

You cannot go back to view the previous screens, as you can when you use a pager program such as less (unless you're using a Terminal window with a sufficient scrollback buffer, that is). cat is mainly used with redirection, as we'll see in a moment.

By the way, if you enter cat without a filename, it tries to read from the keyboard (as we mention earlier). You can get out by pressing Control-D.

When you add > *filename* to the end of a command line, the program's output is diverted from the standard output to the named file. The > symbol is called the *output redirection operator*.

When you use the > operator, be careful not to accidentally overwrite a file's contents. Your system may let you redirect output to an existing file. If so, the old file will be deleted (or, in Unix lingo, "clobbered"). Be careful not to overwrite a much needed file!

Many shells can protect you from this risk. In the *tcsh* shell (the default shell for OS X), use the command set noclobber. The Korn and bash shell command is set -o noclobber. Enter the command at a shell prompt or put it in your shell's startup file. After that, the shell won't allow you to redirect onto an existing file and overwrite its contents.

This doesn't protect against overwriting by Unix programs such as cp; it works only with the > redirection operator. For more protection, you can set Unix file access permissions.

For example, let's use cat with this operator. The file contents that you'd normally see on the screen (from the standard output) are diverted into another file, which we'll then read using cat (without any redirection!):

```
% cat /etc/passwd > mypassword
% cat mypassword
nobody:*:-2:-2:Unprivileged User:/dev/null:/dev/null
root:*:0:0:System Administrator:/var/root:/bin/tcsh
daemon:*:1:1:System Services:/var/root:/dev/null
unknown:*:99:99:Unknown User:/dev/null:/dev/null
www:*:70:70:World Wide Web Server:/Library/WebServer:/dev/null
%
```

An earlier example showed how cat /etc/passwd displays the file */etc/passwd* on the screen. The example here adds the > operator; so the output of cat goes to a file called *mypassword* in the working directory. Displaying the file *mypassword* shows that its contents are the same as the file */etc/passwd* (the effect is the same as the copy command cp /etc/passwd mypassword).

You can use the > redirection operator with any program that sends text to its standard output—not just with cat. For example:

```
% who > users
% date > today
% ls
password    today    users    ...
```

We've sent the output of who to a file called *users* and the output of date to the file named *today*. Listing the directory shows the two new files. Let's look at the output from the who and date programs by reading these two files with cat:

```
% cat users
taylor    console    Feb  5 08:21
taylor    ttyp1      Feb  5 08:47
```

```
% cat today
Tue Feb  5 10:29:00 PST 2002
%
```

You can also use the cat program and the > operator to make a small text file. We told you earlier to type Control-D if you accidentally enter cat without a filename. This is because the cat program alone takes whatever you type on the keyboard as input. Thus, the command:

```
cat > filename
```

takes input from the keyboard and redirects it to a file. Try the following example:

```
% cat > to_do
Finish report by noon
Lunch with Xian
Swim at 5:30
^D
%
```

cat takes the text that you typed as input (in this example, the three lines that begin with Finish, Lunch, and Swim), and the > operator redirects it to a file called *to_do*. Type Control-D *once*, on a new line by itself, to signal the end of the text. You should get a shell prompt.

You can also create a bigger file from smaller files with the cat command and the > operator. The form:

```
cat file1 file2 > newfile
```

creates a file *newfile*, consisting of *file1* followed by *file2*.

```
% cat today to_do > diary
% cat diary
Tue Feb  5 10:29:00 PST 2002
Finish report by noon
Lunch with Xian
Swim at 5:30
%
```

You can't use redirection to add a file to itself, along with other files. For example, you might hope that the following command would merge today's to-do list with tomorrow's. This won't work!

```
% cat to_do to_do.tomorrow > to_do.tomorrow
cat: to_do.tomorrow: input file is output file
```

cat warns you, but it's actually already too late. When you redirect a program's output to a file, Unix empties (clobbers) the file *before* the program starts running. The right way to do this is by using a temporary file (as you'll see in a later example) or simply by using a text editor program.

You can add more text to the end of an existing file, instead of replacing its contents, by using the >> (append redirection) operator. Use it as you would the > (output redirection) operator. So:

    cat *file2* >> *file1*

appends the contents of *file2* to the end of *file1*. For an example, let's append the contents of the file *users* and the current date and time to the file *diary*. Here's what it looks like:

```
% cat users >> diary
% date >> diary
% cat diary
Tue Feb  5 10:29:00 PST 2002
Finish report by noon
Lunch with Xian
Swim at 5:30
taylor    console  Feb  5 08:21
taylor    ttyp1    Feb  5 08:47
Tue Feb  5 10:30:58 PST 2002
%
```

Unix doesn't have a redirection operator that adds text to the beginning of a file. You can do this by storing the new text in a temporary file, then by using a text editor program to read the temporary file into the start of the file you want to edit. You also can do the job with a temporary file and redirection. Maybe you'd like each day's entry to go at the beginning of your *diary* file. Simply rename *diary* to something like *temp*. Make a new *diary* file with today's entries, then append *temp* (with its old contents) to the new *diary*. For example:[*]

```
% mv diary temp
% date > diary
% cat users >> diary
% cat temp >> diary
% rm temp
```

Pipes and Filters

We've seen how to redirect input from a file and output to a file. You can also connect two *programs* together so that the output from one program becomes the input of the next program. Two or more programs connected in this way form a *pipe*. To make a pipe, put a vertical bar (|) on the command line between two commands. When a pipe is set up between two

---

[*] This example could be shortened by combining the two cat commands into one, giving both filenames as arguments to a single cat command. That wouldn't work, though, if you were making a real diary with a command other than cat users.

commands, the standard output of the command to the left of the pipe symbol becomes the standard input of the command to the right of the pipe symbol. Any two commands can form a pipe as long as the first program writes to standard output and the second program reads from standard input.

When a program takes its input from another program, performs some operation on that input, and writes the result to the standard output (which may be piped to yet another program), it is referred to as a *filter*. A common use of filters is to modify output. Just as a common filter culls unwanted items, Unix filters can restructure output.

Most Unix programs can be used to form pipes. Some programs that are commonly used as filters are described in the next sections. Note that these programs aren't used only as filters or parts of pipes. They're also useful on their own.

grep

The grep program searches a file or files for lines that have a certain pattern. The syntax is:

```
grep "pattern" file(s)
```

The name "grep" is derived from the ed (a Unix line editor) command g/re/p, which means "globally search for a regular expression and print all matching lines containing it." A *regular expression* is either some plain text (a word, for example) and/or special characters used for pattern matching. When you learn more about regular expressions, you can use them to specify complex patterns of text.

The simplest use of grep is to look for a pattern consisting of a single word. It can be used in a pipe so only those lines of the input files containing a given string are sent to the standard output. But let's start with an example reading from files: searching all files in the working directory for a word—say, *Unix*. We'll use the wildcard * to quickly give grep all filenames in the directory.

```
% grep "Unix" *
ch01:Unix is a flexible and powerful operating system
ch01:When the Unix designers started work, little did
ch05:What can we do with Unix?
%
```

When grep searches multiple files, it shows the filename where it finds each matching line of text. Alternatively, if you don't give grep a filename to read, it reads its standard input; that's the way all filter programs work:

```
% ls -l | grep "Jan"
drwx------   4 taylor  staff    264 Jan 29 22:33 Movies/
drwx------   2 taylor  staff    264 Jan 13 10:02 Music/
```

```
drwxr-xr-x  12 root    staff   364 Jan  9 20:24 NetInfo/
drwx------  95 taylor  staff  3186 Jan 29 22:44 Pictures/
drwxr-xr-x   3 taylor  staff   264 Jan 24 21:24 Public/
%
```

First, the example runs ls -l to list your directory. The standard output of ls -l is piped to grep, which only outputs lines that contain the string Jan (that is, files or directories that were last modified in January and any other lines that have the pattern "Jan" within). Because the standard output of grep isn't redirected, those lines go to the Terminal screen.

grep options let you modify the search. Table 6-1 lists some of the options.

Table 6-1. Some grep options

Option	Description
-v	Print all lines that do not match pattern.
-n	Print the matched line and its line number.
-l	Print only the names of files with matching lines (lowercase letter "L").
-c	Print only the count of matching lines.
-i	Match either upper- or lowercase.

Next, let's use a regular expression that tells grep to find lines with *root*, followed by zero or more other characters (abbreviated in a regular expression as .*), then followed by Jan:*

```
% ls -l | grep "root.*Jan"
drwxr-xr-x  12 root    staff   364 Jan  9 20:24 NetInfo/
%
```

For more about regular expressions, see the references in the section "Documentation" in Chapter 10.

sort

The sort program arranges lines of text alphabetically or numerically. The following example sorts the lines in the *food* file (from the section "Printing Files" in Chapter 5) alphabetically. sort doesn't modify the file itself; it reads the file and writes the sorted text to the standard output.

```
% sort food
Afghani Cuisine
```

---

* Note that the regular expression for "zero or more characters," .*, is different than the corresponding filename wildcard *. See the section "File and Directory Wildcards" in Chapter 4. We can't cover regular expressions in enough depth here to explain the difference, though more-detailed books do. As a rule of thumb, remember that the first argument to grep is a regular expression; other arguments, if any, are filenames that can use wildcards.

```
Bangkok Wok
Big Apple Deli
Isle of Java
Mandalay
Sushi and Sashimi
Sweet Tooth
Tio Pepe's Peppers
```

By default, sort arranges lines of text alphabetically. Many options control the sorting, and Table 6-2 lists some of them.

Table 6-2. Some sort options

Option	Description
-n	Sort numerically (example: 10 sorts after 2), ignore blanks and tabs.
-r	Reverse the sorting order.
-f	Sort upper- and lowercase together.
+x	Ignore first x fields when sorting.

More than two commands may be linked up into a pipe. Taking a previous pipe example using grep, we can further sort the files modified in January by order of size. The following pipe uses the commands ls, grep, and sort:

```
% ls -l | grep "Jan" | sort +4n
drwx------    2 taylor   staff    264 Jan 13 10:02 Music/
drwx------    4 taylor   staff    264 Jan 29 22:33 Movies/
drwxr-xr-x    3 taylor   staff    264 Jan 24 21:24 Public/
drwxr-xr-x   12 root     staff    364 Jan  9 20:24 NetInfo/
drwx------   95 taylor   staff   3186 Jan 29 22:44 Pictures/
%
```

This pipe sorts all files in your directory modified in January by order of size, and prints them to the Terminal screen. The sort option +4n skips four fields (fields are separated by blanks), then sorts the lines in numeric order. So, the output of ls, filtered by grep, is sorted by the file size (this is the fifth column, starting with 1605). Both grep and sort are used here as filters to modify the output of the ls -l command. If you wanted to email this listing to someone, you could add a final pipe to the mail program. Or you could print the listing by piping the sort output to your printer command (either lp, lpr, or atprint).

Piping to a Pager

The less program, which you saw in the section "Looking Inside Files with less" in Chapter 2, can also be used as a filter. A long output normally zips by you on the screen, but if you run text through less, the display stops after each screenful of text.

Let's assume that you have a long directory listing. (If you want to try this example and need a directory with lots of files, use cd first to change to a system directory such as */bin* or */usr/bin.*) To make it easier to read the sorted listing, pipe the output through less:

```
% ls -l | grep "Jan" | sort +4n | less
drwx------    2 taylor   staff    264 Jan 13 10:02 Music/
drwx------    4 taylor   staff    264 Jan 29 22:33 Movies/
drwxr-xr-x    3 taylor   staff    264 Jan 24 21:24 Public/
drwxr-xr-x   12 root     staff    364 Jan  9 20:24 NetInfo/
   .
   .
   .
drwx------   95 taylor   staff   3186 Jan 29 22:44 Pictures/
:
```

less reads a screenful of text from the pipe (consisting of lines sorted by order of file size), then prints a colon (:) prompt. At the prompt, you can type a less command to move through the sorted text. less reads more text from the pipe and shows it to you and saves a copy of what it has read, so you can go backward to reread previous text if you want. (The simpler pager programs more and pg generally can't back up while reading from a pipe.) When you're done seeing the sorted text, the q command quits less.

Exercise: Redirecting Input/Output

In the following exercises you redirect output, create a simple pipe, and use filters to modify output.

Redirect output to a file.	Enter who > users
Count the number of lines in that file.	Enter wc -l < users
Sort the output of a program.	Enter who	sort
Append sorted output to a file.	Enter who	sort >> users
Display output to the screen.	Enter less users (or more users or pg users)
Display long output to the screen.	Enter ls -l /bin	less (or more or pg)
Format and print a file with pr.	Enter pr users	lp or pr users	lpr

## CHAPTER 7

Accessing the Internet

A network lets computers communicate with each other, sharing files, email, and much more. Unix systems have been networked for more than 25 years, and Macintosh systems have always had networking as an integral part of the system design from the very first system released in 1984.

This chapter introduces Unix networking: running programs on other computers, copying files between computers, browsing the World Wide Web, sending and receiving email messages, reading and posting messages to Usenet "Net news" groups, and "chatting" interactively with other users on your local computer or worldwide.

Remote Logins

The computer you log in to may not be the computer you need to use. For instance, you might have a nifty iMac running Mac OS X on your desk but need to do some work on the main computer in another building. Or you might be a professor doing research with a computer at another university. Your Mac can connect to another Unix computer to let you work as if you were sitting at that computer. You can actually connect to another Mac running Mac OS X (if enabled) too, but you can't run Aqua applications, just the command line. This section describes how to connect to another computer from within the Terminal.

If you'd like to set up your computer to allow remote logins, your best bet is to choose System Preferences from the Mac OS X Apple menu in the top left corner of your screen. Within the Sharing pane, select the Application tab, and you'll find an option "Allow remote login." With that checked, you can log in from home or anywhere else if you know the account and password information.

To log in to a remote computer using Terminal, first log in to your local computer by launching the Terminal application. Then start a program that connects to the remote computer. Some typical programs for connecting over a computer network are telnet, ssh (secure shell), rsh (remote shell), or rlogin (remote login). All of these are supported and included with Mac OS X. In any case, when you log off the remote computer, the remote login program quits and you get another shell prompt from your local computer.

Figure 7-1 shows how remote login programs such as telnet work. In a local login, you interact directly with the shell program running on your local system. In a remote login, you run a remote-access program on your local system; that program lets you interact with a shell program on the remote system.

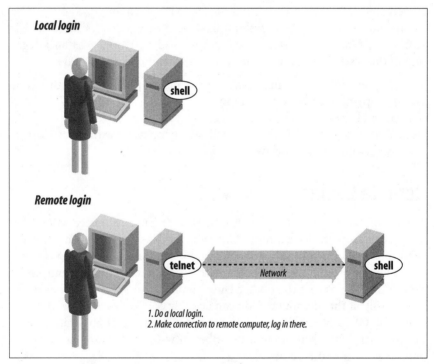

Figure 7-1. Local login, remote login

The syntax for most remote login programs is:

    program-name remote-hostname

For example, when Dr. Nelson wants to connect to the remote computer named *biolab.medu.edu*, she'd first make a local login to her Mac named *fuzzy* by launching Terminal. Next, she'd use the `telnet` program to reach the remote computer. Her session would look something like this:

```
Welcome to Darwin!
fuzzy% telnet biolab.medu.edu

Medical University Biology Laboratory

biolab.medu.edu login: jdnelson
Password:

biolab$
.
.
.
biolab$ exit
Connection closed by foreign host.
fuzzy%
```

Her accounts have shell prompts that include the hostname. This reminds her when she's logged in remotely. If you use more than one system but don't have the hostname in your prompt, see the sections "Customizing Your Session" or "Documentation" to find out how to add it.

 When you're logged on to a remote system, keep in mind that the commands you type will take effect on the remote system, not your local one! For instance, if you use `lpr` to print a file, the printer it comes out of may be very far away.

The programs `rsh` (also called `rlogin`) and `ssh` generally don't give you a `login:` prompt. These programs assume that your remote username is the same as your local username. If they're different, give your remote username on the command line of the remote login program, as shown in the next example.

You may be able to log in without typing your remote password or passphrase.* Otherwise, you'll be prompted after entering the command line.

Following are four sample `ssh` and `rsh` command lines. The first pair shows how to log in to the remote system, *biolab.medu.edu*, when your username is the same on both the local and remote systems. The second pair shows how to log in if your remote username is different (in this case, *jdnelson*); note

---

* In `ssh`, you can run an *agent* program, such as `ssh-agent`, that asks for your passphrase once, then handles authentication every time you run `ssh` or `scp` afterward. For `rsh` and `rcp`, the remote system needs to list your local computer in a file named *hosts.equiv* that's set up by the system administrator.

that the Mac OS X versions of `ssh` and `rsh` may support both syntaxes shown depending on how the remote host is configured:

```
% ssh biolab.medu.edu
% rsh biolab.medu.edu
% ssh jdnelson@biolab.medu.edu
% rsh -l jdnelson biolab.medu.edu
```

About Security

Today's Internet and other public networks have users who try to break into computers and snoop on other network users. While the popular media calls these people *hackers*, most hackers are self-respecting programmers who enjoy pushing the envelope of technology. These evildoers are better known as *crackers*. Most remote login programs (and file transfer programs, which we cover later in this chapter) were designed 20 years ago or more, when networks were friendly places with cooperative users. Those programs (many versions of `telnet` and `rsh`, for instance) make a cracker's job easy. They transmit your data across the network in a way that allows crackers to read it, and they either send your password along, visible to the crackers or expect computers to allow access without passwords.

SSH is different; it was designed with security in mind. If anything you do over a network (such as the Internet) is at all confidential, you really should find SSH programs and learn how to use them. SSH isn't just for Unix systems! There are SSH programs that let you log in and transfer files between Microsoft Windows machines, between Windows and Unix, Mac OS 9, and more. Better, your Mac OS X machine already has SSH installed and ready to run. A good place to get all the details and recommendations for programs is the book *SSH: The Secure Shell*, by Daniel J. Barrett and Richard Silverman (O'Reilly).

Transferring Files

You may need to copy files between computers. For instance, you can put a backup copy of an important file you're editing onto an account at a computer in another building or another city. Dr. Nelson could put a copy of a datafile from her local computer onto a central computer, where her colleagues can access it. Or you might want to download 20 files from an FTP server, but not want to go through the tedious process of clicking on them one by one in a web browser window. If you need to do this sort of thing often, your system administrator may be able to set up a networked filesystem connection; then you'll be able to use local programs such as `cp` and `mv`. But Unix systems also have command-line tools for transferring files between computers. These often work more quickly than graphical tools. We explore them later in this section.

scp and rcp

Mac OS X includes both scp (secure copy) and rcp (remote copy) programs for copying files between two computers. In general, you must have accounts on both computers to use these. The syntax of scp and rcp are similar to cp, but also let you add the remote hostname to the start of a file or directory pathname. The syntax of each argument is:

> hostname:pathname

hostname: is needed only for remote files. You can copy from a remote computer to the local computer, from the local computer to a remote computer, or between two remote computers.

The scp program is much more secure than rcp, so we suggest using scp to transfer private files over insecure networks such as the Internet. For privacy, scp encrypts the file and your passphrase.

For example, let's copy the files *report.may* and *report.june* from your home directory on the computer named *giraffe.intuitive.com* and put the copies into your working directory (.) on the machine you're presently logged in to. If you haven't set up the SSH agent that lets you use scp without typing your passphrase, scp will ask you:

```
% scp giraffe.intuitive.com:report.may giraffe.intuitive.com:report.june .
Enter passphrase for RSA key 'taylor@mac':
```

To use wildcards in the remote filenames, put quotation marks ("*name*") around each remote name.[*] You can use absolute or relative pathnames; if you use relative pathnames, they start from your home directory on the remote system. For example, to copy all files from your *food/lunch* subdirectory on your *giraffe* account into your working directory (.) on the local account, enter:

```
% scp "giraffe.intuitive.com:food/lunch/*" .
```

Unlike cp, the Mac OS X versions of scp and rcp don't have an -i safety option. If the files you're copying already exist on the destination system (in the previous example, that's your local machine), those files are overwritten.

---

[*] Quotes tell the local shell not to interpret special characters, such as wildcards, in the filename. The wildcards are passed, unquoted, to the remote shell, which interprets them *there*.

If your system has rcp, your system administrator may not want you to use it for system security reasons. Another program, ftp, is more flexible and secure than rcp (but much less secure than scp).

FTP

FTP, file transfer protocol, is a standard way to transfer files between two computers. The Unix ftp program does FTP transfers from the command line. Mac OS X also includes a friendlier version of ftp named ncftp, which we'll use later in this chapter. There are also a number of easy-to-use graphical FTP tools available from the Apple web site (go to Get Mac OS X Software... from the Apple menu and click on Internet Tools). But we cover the standard ftp program here. The computers on either end of the FTP connection must be connected by a network (such as the Internet), but they don't need to run Unix.

To start FTP, identify yourself to the remote computer by giving the username and password for your account on that remote system. Unfortunately, sending your username and password over a public network means that snoopers might see them—and use them to log into your account on that system.

A special kind of FTP, *anonymous FTP*, happens if you log in to the remote server with the username *anonymous*. The password is your email address, such as *alex@foo.co.uk*. (The password isn't usually required; it's a courtesy to the remote server.) Anonymous FTP lets anyone log in to a remote system and download publicly accessible files to their local systems.

Command-line ftp

To start the standard Unix ftp program, provide the remote computer's hostname:

```
ftp hostname
```

ftp prompts for your username and password on the remote computer. This is something like a remote login (see the section "Remote Logins," earlier in this chapter), but ftp doesn't start your usual shell. Instead, ftp prints its own prompt and uses a special set of commands for transferring files. Table 7-1 lists the most important ftp commands.

Table 7-1. Some ftp commands

Command	Description
put *filename*	Copies the file *filename* from your local computer to the remote computer. If you give a second argument, the remote copy will have that name.

Table 7-1. Some ftp commands (continued)

Command	Description
mput *filenames*	Copies the named files (you can use wildcards) from the local computer to the remote computer.
get *filename*	Copies the file *filename* from the remote computer to your local computer. If you give a second argument, the local copy will have that name.
mget *filenames*	Copies the named files (you can use wildcards) from the remote computer to the local computer.
prompt	A "toggle" command that turns prompting on or off during transfers with the mget and mput commands. By default, mget and mput will prompt you "mget *filename*?" or "mput *filename*?" before transferring each file; you answer y or n each time. Typing prompt once, from an ftp> prompt, stops the prompting; all files will be transferred without question until the end of the ftp session. Or, if prompting is off, typing prompt at an ftp> prompt resumes prompting.
cd *pathname*	Changes the working directory on the remote machine to *pathname* (ftp typically starts at your home directory on the remote machine).
lcd *pathname*	Changes ftp's working directory on the local machine to *pathname*. (ftp's first local working directory is the same working directory from which you started the program.) Note that the ftp lcd command changes only ftp's working directory. After you quit ftp, your shell's working directory will not have changed.
dir	Lists the remote directory (like ls -l).
binary	Tells ftp to copy the file(s) that follow it without translation. This preserves pictures, sound, or other data.
ascii	Transfers plain-text files, translating data if needed. For instance, during transfers between a Microsoft Windows system (which adds Control-M to the end of each line of text) and a Unix system (which doesn't), an ascii-mode transfer removes or adds those characters as needed.
quit	Ends the ftp session and takes you back to a shell prompt.

Here's an example. Carol uses ftp to copy the file *todo* from her *work* subdirectory on her account on the remote computer *rhino*:

```
% ls
afile    ch2    somefile
% ftp rhino.zoo.edu
Connected to rhino.zoo.edu.
Name (rhino:carol): csmith
Password:
ftp> cd work
ftp> dir
total 3
-rw-r--r--  1 csmith    mgmt     47 Feb  5  2001 for.ed
-rw-r--r--  1 csmith    mgmt    264 Oct 11 12:18 message
-rw-r--r--  1 csmith    mgmt    724 Nov 20 14:53 todo
ftp> get todo
ftp> quit
% ls
afile    ch2    somefile    todo
```

We've explored the most basic ftp commands here. Entering help at an ftp> prompt gives a list of all commands; entering help followed by an ftp command name gives a one-line summary of that command.

NcFTP

While the ftp program is powerful, it's not the most friendly application in the world, even within the Unix space. Indeed, we've long joked that it's the only program in Unix that never turned off "debugging mode." Fortunately, Mac OS X offers a sophisticated and easier alternative from the command line: ncftp. A quick example:

```
% ncftp intuitive.com
NcFTP 2.4.3 (March 19, 1998), by Mike Gleason.
Tip: The "get" command can now fetch whole directories. Try "get -R"
sometime.

Trying to connect to intuitive.com...
Guest login ok, access restrictions apply.
intuitive:/>help get
get: fetches files from the remote host.
Usage: get [-flags] file1 [file2...]
Flags:
  -C   : Force continuation (reget).
  -f   : Force overwrite.
  -G   : Don't use wildcard matching.
  -R   : Recursive.  Useful for fetching whole directories.
  -n X : Get selected files only if X days old or newer.
  -z   : Get the remote file X, and name it to Y.
Examples:
  get README
  get README.*
  get -G **Name.with.stars.in.it**
  get -R new-files-directory
  get -z WIN.INI ~/junk/windows-init-file

intuitive:/> ls -l
total 20
-rw-r--r--    1 root     root        10000 Jul 21  2000 10k.html
dr-xrwxr-x    2 root     root           20 Jan 16  2001 bin/
dr-xrwxr-x    2 root     root            9 Aug  9  1999 dev/
dr-xrwxr-x    2 root     root           38 Jan 15 14:42 etc/
d---------    2 root     root            9 Aug  9  1999 incoming/
dr-xr-xr-x    2 root     root           39 Aug  9  1999 lib/
dr-xr-xr-x    2 root     root           39 Jan  9  2001 lib32/
dr-xrwxr-x   10 root     root          123 Aug  9  1999 pub/
intuitive:/> get 10k.html
Receiving file: 10k.html
100%  0 ===================================> 10000 bytes. ETA:  0:00
10k.html:  10000 bytes received in 1.02 seconds, 9.57 kB/s.
intuitive:/> quit
```

Though the face of ncftp isn't much more attractive than ftp, you can see from the options to the get command that there's a lot more sophistication under the hood. If you expect to use ftp a lot, you'd do well to learn more about ncftp (which you can do by reading the manpage, or reading the online documentation for this great utility at *http://www.ncftp.com/ncftp/*).

SFTP: FTP to secure sites

If you can only use ssh to connect to a remote site, chances are it won't support regular FTP transactions either, probably due to higher security. Mac OS X also includes a version of ftp that works with the standard SSH server programs and works identically to regular FTP. Just type sftp at the command line.

FTP with a web browser

If you need a file from a remote site, and you don't need all the control that you get with the ftp program, you can use a web browser to download files using anonymous FTP. To do that, make a URL (location) with this syntax:

```
ftp://hostname/pathname
```

For instance, *ftp://somecorp.za/pub/reports/2001.pdf* specifies the file *2001.pdf* from the directory */pub/reports* on the host *somecorp.za*. In most cases, you can also start with just the first part of the URL—such as *ftp://somecorp.za*—and browse your way through the FTP directory tree to find what you want. If your web browser doesn't prompt you to save a file, use its Save menu command.

An even faster way to download a file is with the curl (copy from URL) command. For example, to save a copy of the report in the current directory, simply enter:

```
% curl ftp://somecorp.za/pub/reports/2001.pdf
```

Other FTP solutions

One of the pleasures of working with Unix within the Mac OS X environment is that there are a wealth of great Aqua applications. In the world of FTP-based file transfer, the choices are all uniformly excellent, starting with *Fetch*, *NetFinder*, *rbrowser*, and *Anarchie*, and encompassing many other possibilities. Again, either go to the Apple web site "Get Mac OS X Software..." or try the shareware archive site Download.com (*http://www.macosxaps.com/* or *http://www.download.com/*).

Practice

You can practice your ftp and ncftp skills by connection to the public FTP archive *ftp.apple.com*. Log in as *ftp* with your email address as the password, then look around. Try downloading a research paper or document. If you have an account on a remote system, try using ncp and scp to copy files back and forth.

## CHAPTER 8

Unix-Based Internet Tools

If you're going to be interacting with the Internet extensively, odds are good that you'll opt for attractive and easy-to-use Aqua applications. Bear with us, though; there's a lot of power in the Unix command-line alternatives, and they're well worth learning.

Lynx, a Text-Based Web Browser

There are a number of excellent web browsers available within Aqua, including Microsoft Internet Explorer, Mozilla, Omniweb, and Opera. While attractive, graphically based web browsers can be slow—especially with flashy, graphics-laden web pages on a slow network.

The Lynx web browser (originally from the University of Kansas, and available on many Unix systems) is different because it's a text-based web browser that works within the Terminal application. Being text-only causes it to have some tradeoffs you should know about. Lynx indicates where graphics occur in a page layout; you won't see the graphics, but the bits of text that Lynx uses in their place can clutter the screen. Still, because it doesn't have to download or display those graphics, Lynx is *fast*, especially over a dialup modem or busy network connection. Sites with complex multicolumn layouts can be hard to follow with Lynx; a good rule is to page through the screens, looking for the link you want and ignore the rest. Forms and drop-down lists are a challenge at first, but Lynx always gives you helpful hints for forms and lists, as well as other web page elements, in the third line from the bottom of the screen. With those warts (and others), though, once you get a feel for Lynx you may find yourself choosing to use it—even on a graphical system.

Most importantly, Lynx isn't included with the default Mac OS X distribution, even on the Developer CD-ROM. You'll need to go to the "Get Mac

OS X Software..." link off the Apple menu, which opens a web browser and takes you to the Apple web site. From there, find and click on the "Unix Apps & Utilities" link, which then offers a list of useful Unix applications. For now, just download Lynx and run the installer.

With Lynx installed, let's now take a quick tour.

The Lynx command line syntax is:

```
lynx "location"
```

For example, to visit the O'Reilly home page, enter lynx "http://www. oreilly.com" or simply lynx "www.oreilly.com". (It's safest to put quotes around the location, because many URLs have special characters that the shell might interpret otherwise.) Figure 8-1 shows part of the home page.

To move around the Web, Lynx uses your keyboard's arrow keys, spacebar, and a set of single-letter commands. The third line from the bottom of a Lynx screen gives you a hint of what you might want to do at the moment. In Figure 8-1, for instance, "press space for next page" means you can see the next screenful of this web page by pressing the spacebar (at the bottom edge of your keyboard). Lynx doesn't use a scrollbar; instead, use the spacebar to go forward in a page, and use the b command to move back to the previous screenful of the same web page. The bottom two lines of the screen remind you of common commands, and the help system (which you get by typing h) lists the rest.

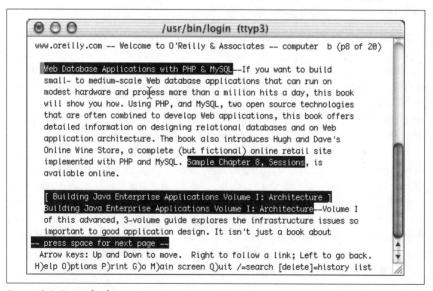

Figure 8-1. Lynx display

The links (which you would click on if you were using a graphical web browser) are highlighted. One of those links is the *currently selected link*, which you can think of as the link where your cursor sits. Depending on how you've configured Terminal, links are either boldfaced or presented in a different color, and the selected link (in Figure 8-1, that's the first: "Web Database Applications with PHP & MySQL") is in reverse video.

When you first view a screen, the link nearest the top is selected. Figure 8-2 shows what you can do at a selected link. To select a later link (farther down the page), press the down-arrow key. The up-arrow key selects the previous link (farther up the page). Once you've selected a link you want to visit, press the right-arrow key to follow that link; the new page appears. Go back to the previous page by pressing the left-arrow key (from any selected link; it doesn't matter which one).

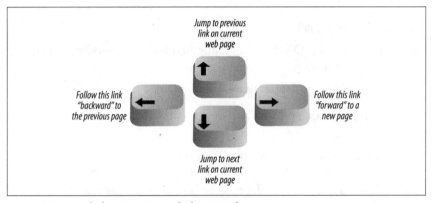

Figure 8-2. Lynx link navigation with the arrow keys

Although Lynx can't display graphics in the Terminal (*no* program can!), it will let you download links that point to graphical files. Then you can use Aqua programs—such as Preview —to view or print those files.

There's much more to Lynx; type H for an overview. Lynx command-line options let you configure almost everything. For a list of options, type man lynx (see the section "Documentation" in Chapter 10) or use:

```
% lynx -help | less
```

Electronic Mail

You may see a notice that says "You have mail" when you first log in to your system, or later, before a shell prompt. Someone has sent you a message or document by *electronic mail* (email). With email, you can compose a message at your terminal and send it to another user or list of users. You also can read any messages that others may have sent to you.

There are a lot of email programs for Unix. If you use email often, we recommend that you start with whatever program other people in your group use.

We start with a brief section on addressing email. Next, you'll see how to send mail from a shell prompt with Berkeley mail. Then we introduce sending and reading mail with Pine, a popular menu-driven program that works without a window system. If you'd like to try a graphical program (which we won't discuss here), there are four standout choices: Mail, included with Mac OS X and written by Apple Computer; Entourage, a part of the Microsoft Office X suite; PowerMail, a fast and efficient option; and Eudora, another popular alternative. All programs' basic principles are the same though, and they all can send and receive messages from each other.

Before we dive into email

Some versions of Mac OS X are misconfigured for command-line email, and if your system behaves similar to this:

```
% mail -s testing taylor@intuitive.com

Just a test message.
.
EOT
% /etc/mail/sendmail.cf: line 81: fileclass: cannot
    open /etc/mail/local-host-names: Group writable directory
```

You need to flip to the Appendix to learn how to make the few changes necessary to fix things. Otherwise, you're ready to continue.

Addressing an Email Message

Most addresses have this syntax:

username@hostname

username is the person's username, such as *jerry*, and *hostname* is either the name of his computer or a central domain name for his entire organization, such as *oreilly.com*. On many Unix systems, if the recipient reads email on the same computer you do, you may omit the *@hostname*. (An easy way to get a copy of a message you send is to add your username to the list of addressees.)

Sending Mail from a Shell Prompt

Mac OS X has a fairly simple program from Berkeley Unix called mail. If you enter the program name at a shell prompt, you can read your email, but its terse interface isn't very friendly. If you enter the program name, followed by an email address or two as arguments, you can send an email message. This is handy for sending a quick message from your keyboard. But it's best used with redirection (explained in Chapter 5) to email the output of a program or the contents of a file.

To send mail, give the address of each person to whom you want to send a message:

```
mail address1 address2 ...
```

 It's best to use simple addresses such as *username@hostname* on the command line. More complex addresses—with peoples' names or special characters such as < and >—can cause trouble unless you know how to deal with them.

After you enter mail and the addresses, if you're sending a message from the keyboard, in most cases the program (depending on how it's set up) prompts you for the subject of the message. The Mac OS X version of the program also accepts a subject as a command-line argument after the -s option; be sure to put quote marks around the subject! Here are two examples of redirection: first, sending the restaurant list you made in an earlier example, then, sorting the list before you send it:

```
% mail -s "My favorite restaurants" taylor@intuitive.com < food
% sort food | mail -s "My favorite restaurants" taylor@intuitive.com
```

If you've redirected the standard input from a pipe or file, as in these two examples, your message will be delivered. Otherwise, mail will wait for you to enter the message body. Type in your message, line by line, pressing Return after every line. When you've finished entering text, type a period followed by a Return or Control-D (just once!) at the start of a new line. You should get the shell prompt at this point, though it might take a few seconds.

```
% mail alicja@moxco.chi.il.us
Subject: My Chicago trip
Alicja, I will be able to attend your meeting.
Please send me the updated agenda.  Thanks.

Dave
.
%
```

If you change your mind before you type the end-of-message dot, you can cancel a message (while you're still entering text) with your interrupt character (see the section "Correcting a Command Line" in Chapter 1). The canceled message may be placed in a file called *dead.letter* in your home directory. To see other commands you can use while sending mail, enter ~?

(tilde, question mark) at the start of a line of your message, then press Return. To redisplay your message after using ~?, enter ~p at the start of a line.

You can't cancel a message after you type dot (unless you're a system administrator and you're lucky to catch the message in time). So, if you change your mind about Alicja's meeting, you'll need to send her another message.

Reading Email with Pine

If you're really set on using a Terminal-based email program, a good choice for upgrading from the stark interface of mail is Pine. Pine is available for download from Apple too: just like Lynx, you'll want to select "Get Mac OS X Software..." from the Apple menu, then click on "Unix Apps & Utilities." Then download Pine and install it.

Pine, from the University of Washington, is a popular program for reading and sending email from a terminal. It works completely from your keyboard; you don't need a mouse.

Start Pine by entering its name at a shell prompt. It also accepts options and arguments on its command line; to find out more, enter pine -h (help). If new email is waiting for you, but you want to experiment with Pine without taking chances, the -o (lowercase letter "O") option makes your inbox folder read-only; you won't be able to change the messages in it until you quit Pine and restart without the -o. Figure 8-3 shows the starting display, the *main menu*.

The highlighted line, which is the default command, gives a list of your email folders.* You can choose the highlighted command by pressing Return, pressing the greater-than sign >, or typing the letter next to it. (Here, this is l—a lowercase L. You don't need to type the commands in uppercase.) But because you probably haven't used Pine before, the only interesting folder is the inbox, which is the folder where your new messages wait for you to read them.

The display in Figure 8-3 shows that there are four messages waiting. Let's go directly to the inbox by pressing I (or by highlighting that line in the menu and pressing Return) to read the new mail. Figure 8-4 has the *message index* for our inbox.

---

* Recent versions of Pine also let you read Usenet newsgroups. The L command takes you to another display where you choose the source of the folders, *then* you see the list of folders from that source. See the section "Usenet News."

Figure 8-3. Pine main menu

Figure 8-4. Pine message index

The main part of the window is a list of the messages in the folder, one message per line. If a line starts with N, as the second message does, it's a new message that hasn't been read. (The first message has been sitting in the inbox for some time now.) Next on each line is the *message number*; messages in a folder are numbered 1, 2, and so on. That's followed by the date the message was sent, who sent it, the number of characters in the message (size), and, finally, the message subject.

At the bottom of the display is Pine's reminder list of commands. When you aren't sure what to do, this is a good place to look. If you don't see what you want here, pressing O (the letter "o"; lowercase is fine) shows you more choices. For more information, ? gives detailed help.

Let's skip this first message and read the next one, number 2. The down-arrow key or the N key moves the highlight bar over that message. As usual, you can get the default action—the one shown in brackets at the bottom of the display (here, [ViewMsg])—by pressing Return or >. The message from Mary Lea will appear.

Just as > took us forward in Pine, the < key generally takes you back to where you came from—in this case, the message index. You can type R to reply to this message, F to forward it (send it on to someone else), D to mark it for deletion, and the Tab key to go to the next message without deleting this one.

When you mark a message for deletion, it stays in the folder message index, marked with a D at the left side of its line, until you quit Pine. Type Q to quit. Pine asks if you really want to quit. If you've marked messages for deletion, Pine asks if you want to *expunge* ("really delete") them. Answering Y here deletes the message.

There's much more to Pine than we can cover here. For instance, it lets you organize mail in multiple folders, print, pipe (output) messages to Unix programs, search for messages, and more. The Mac OS X version of Pine can access mail folders on other computers using IMAP; this lets you use Pine (and other email programs) on many computers, but keep one main set of mail folders on a central computer.

Sending Email with Pine

If you're sending a quick message from a shell prompt, you may want to use the method shown in the section "Sending Mail from a Shell Prompt" earlier in this chapter. For a more interactive way to send email, try Pine. We'll take a quick tour.

If you've already started Pine, you can compose a message from many of its displays by typing C. (Though, as always, not every Pine command is available at every display.) You can also start from the main menu. Or, at a shell prompt, you can go straight into message composition by typing pine *addr1 addr2*, where each *addr* is an email address such as *jerry@oreilly.com*. In that case, after you've sent the mail message, Pine quits and leaves you at another shell prompt.

When you compose a message, Pine puts you in a window called the *composer*. (You'll also go into the composer if you use the Reply or Forward commands while you're reading another mail message.) The composer is a lot like the Pico editor, but the first few lines are special because they're the message *header*—the "To:," "Cc:" (courtesy copy), "Attchmnt:" (attached file), and "Subject:" lines. Figure 8-5 shows an example, already filled in.

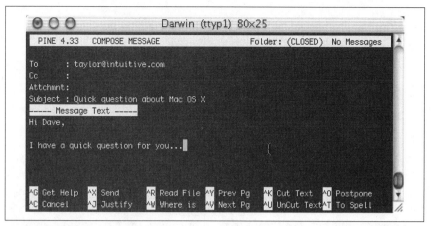

Figure 8-5. Pine composer

As you fill in the header, the composer works differently than when you're in the message text (body of the message). The list of commands at the bottom of the window is a bit different in those cases, too. For instance, while you edit the header, you can attach a file to the end of the message with the "Attach" command, which is Control-J. However, when you edit the body, you can read a file into the place you're currently editing (as opposed to attaching it) with the Control-R "Read File" command. But the main difference between editing the body and the header is the way you enter addresses.

If you have more than one address on the same line, separate them with commas (,). Pine will rearrange the addresses so there's just one on each line.

There are several ways to give the composer the addresses where the message should be sent:

- Type the full email address, for example, *taylor@intuitive.com*.
- If you're sending email to someone who uses the same computer you do, type their username. Pine will fill in *@hostname* as soon as you move the cursor to the next line.
- Type a nickname from the address book. (See the section "Pine address book" later in this chapter.)

Move up and down between the header lines with Control-N and Control-P, or with the up-arrow and down-arrow keys. When you move into the message body (under the "Message Text" line), type any text you want. Paragraphs are usually separated with single blank lines.

If you put a file in your home directory named *.signature* (the name starts with a dot, .), the composer automatically adds its contents to the end of every message you compose. (Some other Unix email programs work the same way.) You can make this file with a text editor such as Pico, or from the Pine setup menu (see the section "Configuring Pine" later in this chapter). It's good Internet etiquette to keep this file short—no more than four or five lines, if possible.

You can use Pico commands such as Control-J to justify a paragraph and Control-T to check your spelling. When you're done, Control-X (exit) leaves the composer, asking first if you want to send the message you just wrote. Or Control-C cancels the message, though you'll be asked if you're sure. If you need to quit but don't want to send or cancel, the Control-O command postpones your message; then, the next time you try to start the composer, Pine asks whether you want to continue the postponed composition.

Pine address book

The Pine *address book* can hold peoples' names and addresses, as well as a *nickname* for each person. When you compose a message, enter a nickname in the message header, Pine replaces that with the full name and address.*

You can enter information by hand from the main menu by choosing A (address book), then adding new entries and editing old ones. Also, as you read email messages that you've received, the T (take address) command makes new address book entries for that message's addressees.

Figure 8-6 shows the address book entry form. Edit each line as you would in the composer, then use Control-X to save the entry. The "Fcc" line gives the name of an optional Pine folder; when you send a message to this address book entry, Pine puts a copy in this folder. (If you leave "Fcc" blank, Pine uses the *sent-mail* folder.) All lines except nickname and address are optional.

Once you've saved that address book entry, if you go into the composer and type the nickname *Jerry*, here's the header you get automatically:

```
To      : Jerry Peek <jpeek@jpeek.com>
Cc      :
Fcc     : authors
Attchmnt:
Subject :
```

---

* The Mac OS X version of Pine also let you store your address book on a central server, in order
for you to access it from whatever other computer you're using at the moment, via IMAP.

Figure 8-6. Pine address book entry

Configuring Pine

The Pine main menu has a Setup entry for configuring Pine. We assume that your system staff has configured important options, such as your printer command, and we look at a few other settings you might want to change.

After you enter S (the "Setup" command), you can choose what kind of setup you want. From the setup screen, you can get to the option configuration area with C (the "Config" command).

The configuration screen has page after page of options. You can look through them with the spacebar (to move forward one page), the - key (back one page), the N key (to move forward to the next entry), and the P key (back to the previous entry). If you know the name of an option you want to change, you can search for it with W (the "Whereis" command).

When you highlight an option, the menu of commands at the bottom of the screen will show you what can do with that particular option. A good choice, while you're exploring, is the ? (help) command, to find out about the option you've highlighted. There are several kinds of options:

- Options with variable values: names of files, hostnames of computers, and so on. For example, the personal-name option sets the name used in the "From:" header field of mail messages you send. The setup entry looks like this:

      personal-name   = <No Value Set: using "Robert L. Stevenson">

  "No Value Set" can mean that Pine is using the default from the system-wide settings, as it is here. If this user wants his email to come from

"Bob Stevenson," he could use the C (Change Val) command to set that name.

- Options that set preferences for various parts of Pine. For instance, the enable-sigdashes option in the "Composer Preferences" section puts two dashes and a space on the line before your default signature. The option line looks like this:

  ```
  [X]  enable-sigdashes
  ```

  The X means that this preference is set, or "on." If you want to turn this option off, use the X (Set/Unset) command to toggle the setting.

- Options for which you can choose one of many possible settings. The option appears as a series of lines. For instance, the first few lines of the saved-msg-name-rule option look like this:

  ```
  saved-msg-name-rule    =
           Set    Rule Values
           ---    ----------------------
           (*)    by-from
           ( )    by-nick-of-from
           ( )    by-nick-of-from-then-from
           ( )    by-fcc-of-from
           ( )    by-fcc-of-from-then-from
  ```

- The * means that the saved-msg-name-rule option is currently set to by-from. (Messages will be saved to a folder named for the person who sent the message.) If you wanted to choose a different setting—for instance, by-fcc-of-from—you'd move the highlight to that line and use the * (Select) command to choose that setting.

  These settings are trickier than the others, but the built-in help command ? explains each choice in detail. Start by highlighting the option name (here, saved-msg-name-rule) and reading its help info. Then look through the settings' names, highlight one you might want, and read its help info to see if it's right for you.

When you exit the setup screen with the E command, Pine asks you to confirm whether you want to save any option changes you made. Answer N if you were just experimenting or aren't sure.

Exercise: Sending and Reading Mail

You can practice sending and reading mail in this exercise:

List logged-in users.	Enter who
Choose a user you know (or choose yourself) send a short message to that person using mail or your favorite email program.	Enter mail *username* or pine *username* or …
Read the message or messages you got.	Enter pine or start your favorite email program; use its "read message" commands.

Reply to one of the messages. (It's okay to reply to a message from yourself.)	Press R in pine or use your email program's "reply" command. Send the completed reply.
Forward one of the messages. (It's okay to forward a message to yourself.)	Press F in pine or use your email program's "forward" command. Add a sentence or two of explanation above the forwarded message. Send the completed message.

Usenet News

Usenet, also called "Net News," has thousands of worldwide discussion groups. Each discussion is carried on as a series of messages in its own *newsgroup*. A newsgroup is named for the kind of discussion that happens there. Each message is a lot like an email message. But, instead of being sent to a list of email addresses, a newsgroup message is sent to all the computers that subscribe to that particular newsgroup—and any user with access to that computer can read and reply to the message.

> Because Usenet is a public forum, you'll find a variety of people with a variety of opinions—some impolite, rude, or worse. Although most users are friendly and helpful, a few people seem to cause most of the problems. Until you're accustomed to Usenet, be aware that you may be offended by some contributors and attacked ("flamed") by others.

To read Usenet groups, you'll need a *newsreader* program, also called a *news client*. Many email programs can read news, too. You can use any newsreader; the principles of all are about the same. Some of the more popular Unix newsreaders are slrn, nn, and trn. We show how to read news with Pine Version 4.33. If you haven't used Pine before, please read the section "Reading Email with Pine" earlier in this chapter.

If your system's copy of Pine has been set up to read Usenet messages, when you choose the L key ("folder list") from the main menu, you'll get a Collection List screen, as shown in Figure 8-7. A *collection* is a group of folders. A collection can be email folders from your local computer, email folders from other computers, or Usenet newsgroup folders. Figure 8-7 shows two collections: *Mail* and *news on news/nntp*. The news collection is selected (highlighted).

If your copy of Pine is recent enough to read Usenet, but doesn't seem to do it, check the configuration settings, as described in the section "Configuring Pine" earlier in this chapter. The collectionList settings can set up a collection of folders for news. You may also need to set the nntp-server hostname to the computer that serves news articles; your system administrator or ISP should be able to tell you the right hostname.

Figure 8-7. Pine Collection List screen

When you press Return or > to view that collection, you'll get a list of newsgroup folders that's probably huge. Usenet has something for everyone! The Pine D command will delete a newsgroup from your list; it won't appear anymore unless you use the A command to add it back. (Pine also has some advanced features, such as "zooming" to a list of folders that you've defined. See the Pine help system for details.) Figure 8-8 shows a list of newsgroups.

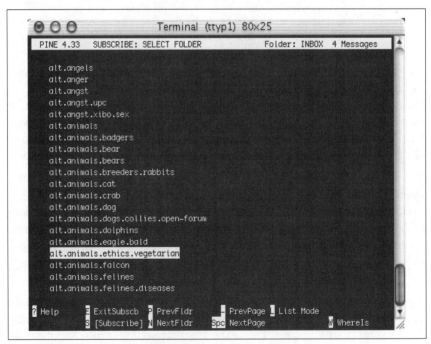

Figure 8-8. Pine newsgroup collection list screen

Newsgroup names are in a hierarchy, with the levels separated by dots (.):

- The main hierarchies include *comp* (for discussions about computers); organization, city, regional, and national groups (such as *ne* for New England, *uk* for the United Kingdom, and so on); *misc* (miscellaneous); and so on. The *alt* (alternative) hierarchy is for almost anything that doesn't fit in the others.

- All the top levels have subcategories, or second-level categories. For instance, the *alt* category has subcategories *alt.angels*, *alt.angers*, *alt.animals*, and so on, as you can see in Figure 8-8.

- A second-level category may have third-level categories. For instance, the category *alt.animals* is divided into *alt.animals.dogs*, *alt.animals.dolphins*, and so on.

When you first start to read Usenet, it's a good idea to spend a couple of hours exploring what's available and what you're interested in, and deleting unwanted newsgroups from your list. The time you spend at first will pay you back later, by letting you go straight to the newsgroups in which you're interested.

People all over the world frequent particular newsgroups. Just as mail folders have email messages, newsgroups have *news articles* (individual messages posted by someone). These messages expire after a period of time. (That's one reason why a lot of newsgroups appear empty.) Let's look into a newsgroup. Go to the newsgroup *news.announce.newusers*; scroll through the folder list by pressing the spacebar, or if in a hurry, use the W (Whereis) command and enter the newsgroup name. Once you've selected the name from the collection list, press Return or > to view it. You'll see a list of messages in the group, as in Figure 8-9.

Figure 8-9. Pine newsgroup message index screen

Read Usenet messages just as you read email messages; for example, select a message from the message index and press Return or > to view it. It stays in the index until it's deleted or expires. Deleting messages you've read or don't want to see makes it easier to find new messages that come in later. To keep a message, save a copy to a Pine mail folder with the S (save) command, email a copy to other users with the F (forward) command, or save a copy to a file with the E (export) command.

 Remember that people worldwide will see your message and have your email address. If your message is insulting, long and rambling, includes a lot of the original message unnecessarily, or just makes people unhappy, you're likely to get a lot of email about it. Many newsgroups have periodic FAQ (frequently asked questions) postings that give more information about the group and answer common questions. We suggest that you not post messages to newsgroups until you've read Usenet for a while, have learned what style is acceptable, and have seen enough of the discussion in a particular group to know whether your question or comment has been discussed recently.

If there's a message you want to reply to, the Pine R command starts a reply. After asking whether to include a copy of the original message in your reply, Pine asks you: "Follow-up to news group(s), Reply via email to author or Both?" If you want all who read this newsgroup to see your reply, choose F to follow up; your reply, including your name and email address, is posted for everyone to see. If your message is just for the author—for instance, a question or a comment—replying by email with R is the better choice.

 Remember that spammers (people who send "junk email" with advertising and worse) will be able to see the email address on your Usenet posting. For that reason, many people set a different email address in the "From:" field when posting Usenet messages. If your Internet provider gives you multiple email addresses, you could choose one just for your Usenet postings. (Readers may want to reply to your message by email, though, so consider using an email address that you do read occasionally. You also can include your "real" address in the body of the article, possibly disguised to fool spammers who search Usenet articles for email addresses.)

You can post a new message to a newsgroup with the C (compose) command. If you're viewing a news folder, Pine asks if you want to compose a message to that newsgroup. (If you answer N (no), Pine creates a regular email message.)

Here's one more tip: to read expired messages or search through years of archives, web sites such as Google Groups (*http://groups.google.com/*) allow this.

Interactive Chat

Need a quick answer from another user without sending an email message and waiting for his reply? Want to have a conversation with your Internet-connected friend in Chile but don't have money for an international phone call? An interactive chat program lets you type text to another user and see her reply moments later. Chatting, or "instant messaging," has become popular. Widely known chat programs are available for Unix; as of this writing, those include Jabber and AOL Instant Messenger. Other programs have been available on Unix systems for years and are included with Mac OS X. We look at two of these: talk and IRC.

talk

The talk program is simple to use. Give the username (and, optionally, the hostname) of the person with whom you want to chat. Then talk will try to notify that person as well as show how to use talk to complete the connection with you. Both of your terminal windows will be split into two sections, one for the text you type and the other for the text you get from the other person. You can type messages back and forth until one of you uses Control-C to break the session.

One advantage of talk is its simplicity; if each of you has a terminal window open, either of you can run the program at any time; if the other person is logged in, he is notified that you want to chat and told how to complete the connection. If both people want to use talk on the same computer—even if one of them is logged in remotely (see the section, "Remote Logins")—it should work well. Unfortunately, there are several talk versions that don't work with each other. So, the first time you try to chat with someone on another host, which might have another talk version (or other problems), it can take planning. Use an email message or phone call to alert them that you'll try talking soon, then experiment to be sure that both of you have compatible talk systems. After that, you're all set.

Here's the syntax:

```
talk username@hostname
```

If the other user is logged onto the same computer as you, omit the *@hostname*. After you run that command, your screen clears with a line of dashes across the middle. The top half shows text you type and informational messages about the connection. The bottom half shows what the other user types.

For example, if your username is *juan*, you're logged onto the computer *sandya.unm.edu*, and you want to talk to the user *ana* at the computer *cielo.cl*, you would type `talk  ana@cielo.cl`. If the connection works, your screen clears and you'll see something like:

```
[No connection yet]
[Waiting for your party to respond]
[Waiting for your party to respond]
[Connection established]
Hi, Ana! Need any help with your exam?
```

The message [Waiting for your party to respond] means that your talk program has found *ana*'s system and is waiting for her to respond. Ana's terminal bell should ring and she should see a message like this in one of her terminal windows:

```
Message from Talk_Daemon@sandya.unm.edu at 18:57 ...
talk: connection requested by juan@sandya.unm.edu.
talk: respond with:  talk juan@sandya.unm.edu
```

If she answers by typing `talk juan@sandya.unm.edu`, the connection should be completed, and her screen should clear and look like Juan's. What she types appears on the top half of her screen and the bottom half of Juan's, and vice versa. It's not always easy to know when the other person has finished typing; one convention is to type o (for "over") when you want a response; type oo (for "over and out") when you're finished. The conversation goes on until one person types Control-C to actually break the connection.

Unfortunately, because there are several versions of talk, and because other things can go wrong, you may see other messages from the talk program. One common message is [Checking for invitation on caller's machine], which usually means that you won't be able to connect. If this happens, it's possible that one system has other versions of the talk program that will work with the particular system to which you're trying to connect—try the ntalk program, for instance. It might also be easier to use a more flexible chat system, such as IRC.

IRC

Internet Relay Chat (IRC) is a long-established system for chatting with other users worldwide. IRC is fairly complex, with some rules you need to understand before using it. We give a brief introduction here; for more details, see *http://www.irchelp.org*. Mac OS X, by default, doesn't include an

IRC client, so you'll need to download one. For a good place to start, download the Fink package management system (from *http://fink.sourceforge.net/*), install it, then at the Terminal command line type `fink install ircii` to install ircII.

Introducing IRC

Unlike the `talk` program, IRC programs let you talk with multiple users on multiple channels. Channels have names, usually starting with #, such as *#football*. (You might hope that a channel name would tell you what sort of discussions happen there, but you'd often be wrong!) Many channels are shared between multiple servers on an IRC *net*, or network; you connect your IRC program to a nearby server, which spreads your channel to other servers around the Net. Some channel names start with &; these channels are local to their server, and not shared around the Net. Finally, you can meet a user from a channel and have a private conversation, a "DCC chat," that doesn't go through servers.

Each user on a channel has a *nick*, or nickname, which is up to nine characters long. It's a good idea to choose a unique nick. Even when you do, if someone else with the same nick joins a channel before you do, you must choose another nick.

Two kinds of users are in control of each channel. *Ops*, or channel operators, choose which other users can join a channel (by "banning" some users from joining) and which users have to leave (by "kicking off" those users). If a channel is empty, the first user to join it is automatically the channel op. (As you can imagine, this system means that some ops can be arbitrary or unhelpful. If an op treats you badly, though, you can just go join another of the thousands of IRC channels.) *IRC ops*, on the other hand, are technical people in charge of the servers themselves; they don't get involved with "people issues."

IRC not only lets you chat; it lets you share files with other users. This can be helpful, but it also can be dangerous; see the warning later in this section.

There are many IRC programs, or "clients," for different operating systems. They all work with each other, though some have more features. The best known Unix program is ircII, which you run by typing `irc`. Another well-liked program, based on ircII, is bitchx; get it from *http://www.bitchx.org*. Many programs can be modified by using *scripts* or *bots*; there are thousands of these floating around IRC. But we advise you to use only well-known programs, and to avoid scripts and bots, unless you know that they're safe.

IRC started long before graphical programs were popular. IRC programs use commands that start with a slash (/), such as /join #football or /whois StevieNix. Some IRC programs have buttons and menus that run commands without typing, but you'll probably find that learning the most common commands is easy—and makes chatting faster, overall, than using a mouse.

IRC can be a wide-open security hole if you don't use it carefully. If you type the wrong command or use an insecure program or script, any user can take over your account, delete all your files, and more. Be careful!

IRC programs can be corrupted; scripts and bots can easily do damage. Even if you think that one is widely known and safe, it can contain a few lines of dangerous "trojan horse" code added by an unscrupulous user. Also, never type a command that another IRC user suggests unless you're sure you know what it does; /load and /dcc get can be especially dangerous.

Finally, you should know that IRC users can get information about you with the /whois *nick* command, where *nick* is your current nick. They'll see your real name unless you set the IRCNAME environment variable to another name (and log in to your system again to make the change take effect). This is explained in the section "Customizing Your Account" in Chapter 2. (By the way, use /whois with your nick to find out what other people can see about you.)

A sample IRC session

When you type irc, your terminal screen splits into two parts. The top part shows what's happening on the server and the channel; the bottom part (a single line) is where you type commands and text. In between the two parts is a status line with the time of day, your nick, and other information. Some terminals can't do what irc wants them to; if you get an error message about this, try the command irc -d to use "dumb mode" instead.

A good ircII command to start with is /help, which provides a list of other commands. The commands /help intro and /help newuser give introductions. For help with a particular command, give its name—such as /help server for help with the /server command. When you're done with help, you'll get a Help? prompt; you can type another help topic name, or simply press Return to leave the help system. Another common command is /motd, the "message of the day," which often explains the server's policies.

You can type your nick on the `irc` command line. Your IRC program should have a default server. You can change servers with the `/server` command; you'd do this if your server is full (you get the message "connection timed out," "connection refused," etc.). If your default IRC server is down or busy, you can also give a server hostname on the `irc` command line, after your nick.

In the following examples, we show the text you type (from the bottom line of the screen) in **boldface**, followed by the responses you might see (from the top of the screen) in unbolded text.

We used these commands:

```
% setenv IRCNAME "Steve St. John"
% irc sstjohn us.undernet.org
*** Connecting to port 6667 of server us.undernet.org
...
*** Closing Link: sstjohn by austin.tx.us.undernet.org (Sorry, your
+connection class is full - try again later or try another server)
*** Connecting to port 6667 of server us.undernet.org
...
*** Welcome to the Internet Relay Network sstjohn (from
+Arlington.VA.US.Undernet.Org)
...
*** on 1 ca 1(4) ft 10(10)

/motd
*** The message of the day was last changed: 22/12/2001
*** on 1 ca 1(4) ft 10(10)
*** - Arlington.VA.US.Undernet.Org Message of the Day -
*** - 27/7/2001 20:39
...
*** -          SERVER POLICIES:
...

/help newuser
*** Help on newuser
...
*** Hit any key for more, 'q' to quit ***
...
Help? Return

/whois sstjohn
*** sstjohn is ~jpeek@kumquat.jpeek.com (Steve St. John)
*** on irc via server *.undernet.org (The Undernet Underworld)
*** sstjohn has been idle 1 minutes
```

Messages from the server start with ***. Long lines are broken and continue on following lines that start with +. After connecting to the server, we used /whois with our nick to find what information other users could see about us. The Undernet servers have thousands of channels open, so we started by searching for channels with "help" in their names; you can use wildcards, such as *help*, to do this:

```
/list *help*
*** Channel    Users  Topic
*** #helpmania 2      A yellow light, an open door, hello neighbor,
+there's room for more. English
*** #underneth 14     -= UndernetHelp =- Ask your color free questions
+& wait for it to be answered. (undernethelp@fivemile.org)
*** #mIRCHelp  14     Welcome to Undernet's mIRC Help Channel! Beginners
+welcome :-)
*** #irc_help  48     Welcome to #irc_help. We do not assist in
+questions/channels regarding warez, mp3, porn, fserve, etc.
...list goes on and on...

/list *mp3*
...list of groups discussing/sharing MP3 files...
```

We want to see what's happening, so we join the biggest help channel: *#irc_help*, which has 48 users now:

```
/join #irc_help
*** sstjohn (jpeek@kumquat.jpeek.com) has joined channel #irc_help
*** Topic for #irc_help: Welcome to #irc_help. We do not assist in
+questions/channels regarding warez, mp3, porn, fserve, etc.
*** Users on #irc_help: sstjohn ChuckieCheese Dodgerl GooberZ
+Kinger MotorMouth @theDRJoker MrBean SweetPea LavaBoy GrandapaJoe
...
```

Some names in the list of users, such as *@Darkmind*, start with @; these users are ops. Let's watch some more of the action. After a couple of users leave the channel, a new user *MsTiger* joins and asks for help. Each time a user types a line of text that isn't a command, it's sent to everyone else on the channel, preceded by that user's nick, such as <MsTiger>:

```
*** ChuckieCheese has left channel #irc_help
*** GooberZ has left channel #irc_help
*** HelloWorld (~hw@foo.edu) has joined channel #irc_help
*** MsTiger (~tiger@zz.ro) has joined channel #irc_help
<MsTiger> help me
<MsTiger> please
<Kinger> MsTiger what can we help you with ?
<MsTiger> my channel is not op
<Kinger> LavaBoy tell MsTiger about no opers
<LavaBoy> MsTiger, *shrug*
<GrandapaJoe> MsTiger Sorry, but there are currently NO IRC Operators
+available to help you with your channels. Please be patient and wait
+for an Operator to join.
*** MsTiger has left channel #irc_help
```

The channel has gotten quiet, so we jump in with a question:

```
Hello all.  When I joined, I had a problem
  ...
Any suggestions??
*** Thor (dfdddd@194.999.231.00) has joined channel #irc_help
<[Wizard]> Can you help me plz
<LavaBoy> Try typing !help in the channel, [MORTAL].
/leave
*** sstjohn has left channel #irc_help
/quit
%
```

No one had an answer, so we left the channel after a few minutes of waiting. Other channels might be a lot livelier and might have had someone willing to chat about my question, but we left the irc program by typing /quit. Then we got another shell prompt.

## CHAPTER 9

Multitasking

Unix can do many jobs at once, dividing the processor's time between the tasks so quickly that it looks as if everything is running at the same time. This is called *multitasking*.

With a window system, you can have many applications running at the same time, with many windows open. But Mac OS X, like most Unix systems, also lets you run more than one program inside the same terminal. This is called *job control*. It gives some of the benefits of window systems to users who don't have windows. But, even if you're using a window system, you may want to use job control to do several things inside the same terminal window. For instance, you may prefer to do most of your work from one terminal window, instead of covering your desktop with multiple windows.

Why else would you want job control? Suppose you're running a program that will take a long time to process. On a single-task operating system such as MS-DOS, you would enter the command and wait for the system prompt to return, telling you that you could enter a new command. In Unix, however, you can enter new commands in the "foreground" while one or more programs are still running in the "background."

When you enter a command as a background process, the shell prompt reappears immediately so that you can enter a new command. The original program will still run in the background, but you can use the system to do other things during that time. Depending on your system and your shell, you may even be able to log off and let the background process run to completion.

Running a Command in the Background

Running a program as a background process is most often done to free a terminal when you know the program will take a long time to run. It's also used whenever you want to launch a new window program from an existing terminal window—so that you can keep working in the existing terminal, as well as in the new window.

To run a program in the background, add the & character at the end of the command line before you press the Return key. The shell then assigns and displays a process ID number for the program:

```
% sort bigfile > bigfile.sort &
[1] 29890
%
```

(Sorting is a good example because it can take a while to sort huge files, so users often do it in the background.)

The process ID (PID) for this program is 29890. The PID is useful when you want to check the status of a background process, or if you need to cancel it. You don't need to remember the PID, because there are Unix commands (explained in the next section) to check on the processes you have running. Some shells write a status line to your screen when the background process finishes.

Here's another example. Mac OS X has a command called open that lets you launch Aqua applications from the Unix command line. You can also feed specific files or directories to the open program, in which case it will launch the appropriate Aqua application that can view or display the file (similarly to double-clicking on the file icon in the Finder). For example, to view the *Library* directory in the Finder, you can use open /Library, but since you want to have it immediately move into the background you need to append the & suffix:

```
% open /Library &
[1] 505
```

A new Finder window will open up, showing the contents of *Library*.

In the C shell, you can put an entire sequence of commands separated by semicolons (;) into the background by putting an ampersand at the end of the entire command line. In other shells, enclose the command sequence in parentheses before adding the ampersand. For instance, you might want to sort a file, then print it after sort finishes. The syntax that works on all shells is:

```
(command1; command2) &
```

The examples above work on all shells. Mac OS X Unix shells also have a feature we mentioned earlier called *job control*. You can use the *suspend character* (usually Control-Z) to suspend a program running in the foreground. The program pauses, and you get a new shell prompt. You can then do anything else you like, including putting the suspended program into the background using the bg command. The fg command brings a suspended or background process to the foreground.

For example, you might start sort running on a big file, and, after a minute, want to send email. Stop sort, then put it in the background. The shell prints a message, then another shell prompt. Send mail while sort runs.

```
% sort hugefile1 hugefile2 > sorted
...time goes by...
CTRL-Z Stopped
% bg
[1]     sort hugefile1 hugefile2 > sorted &
% mail taylor@intuitive.com
```

Checking on a Process

If a background process takes too long, or you change your mind and want to stop a process, you can check the status of the process and even cancel it.

ps

When you enter the command ps, you can see how long a process has been running, the process ID of the background process, and the terminal from which it was run. The tty program shows the name of the Terminal where it's running; this is especially helpful when you're using a window system or you're logged into multiple terminals, as the following code shows:

```
% ps
  PID TT  STAT    TIME COMMAND
  310 std S    0:00.37 -tcsh (tcsh)
  510 std R+   0:00.00 ps
  459 p2  S+   0:00.25 -tcsh (tcsh)
% tty
/dev/ttyp1
```

In its basic form, ps lists the following:

Process ID (PID)
  A unique number assigned by Unix to the process.

Terminal name (TT)
  The Unix name for the terminal from which the process was started.

Run Time State (STAT)
  The current state of each job. "S" is sleeping, "R" is runnable, "T" is stopped, and "I" is idle (sleeping for more than 20–30 seconds). Additionally, state can include "+" to indicate it's part of the foreground

group process, "E" indicates the process is exiting, and "W" means it's swapped out.*

Run time (TIME)

The amount of computer time (in minutes and seconds) that the process has used.

Command (CMD)

The name of the process.

Each terminal window has its own terminal name. The previous code shows processes running on two windows: *std* and *p2*. The Mac OS X version of ps lists only the processes on the same terminal where you run ps; other versions list processes on all terminals where you're logged in. If you have more than one terminal window open, but all the entries in the TT column show the same terminal name, try typing ps -u *username*, where *username* is your username. If you need to find out the name of a particular terminal, run the tty program from a shell prompt in that window.

If you have ps show you all the processes running, you will see quite a few processes you don't recognize; they're helping Aqua do its job. You may also see the names of any other programs running in the background and the name of your shell's process (sh, csh, and so on)—although the Mac OS X version of ps shows all processes by default. ps may or may not list its own process.

You can also specify process ID values to ps to find out about specific jobs. Consider the following:

```
% sort verybigfile > big-sorted-output
[1]  522
% ps 522
  PID  TT  STAT      TIME COMMAND
  522 std  R      0:00.32 sort verybigfile
% ps $$
  PID  TT  STAT      TIME COMMAND
  310 std  S      0:00.41 -tcsh (tcsh)
```

As the last command shows, you can easily ascertain what command shell you're running at any time by using the $$ shortcut for the process ID of the current shell. Feed that to ps, and it'll tell you about the shell process you're running.

You should be aware that there are two types of programs on Unix systems: directly executable programs and interpreted programs. Directly executable programs are written in a programming language such as C and stored in a

---

* The ps manpage has details on all possible states for a process. It's quite interesting reading.

file that the system can read directly. Interpreted programs, such as shell scripts and Perl scripts, are sequences of commands that are read by an interpreter program. If you execute an interpreted program, you will see an additional command (such as perl, sh, or csh) in the ps listing, as well as any Unix commands that the interpreter is executing currently.

Shells with job control have a command called jobs that lists background processes started from that shell. As mentioned earlier, there are commands to change the foreground/background status of jobs. There are other job control commands as well. See the references in the section "Documentation" in Chapter 10.

Canceling a Process

You may decide that you shouldn't have put a process in the background or the process is taking too long to execute. You can cancel a background process if you know its process ID.

kill

The kill command terminates a process. The command's format is:

    kill PID(s)

kill terminates the designated process IDs (shown under the PID heading in the ps listing). If you do not know the process ID, do a ps first to display the status of your processes.

In the following example, the sleep *n* command simply causes a process to "go to sleep" for *n* seconds. We enter two commands, sleep and who, on the same line, as a background process.

```
% (sleep 60; who)&
[1] 543
% ps
  PID  TT  STAT      TIME COMMAND
  310 std  S      0:00.52 -tcsh (tcsh)
  543 std  S      0:00.00 -tcsh (tcsh)
  544 std  S      0:00.01 sleep 60
  545 std  R+     0:00.00 ps
  459  p2  S+     0:00.25 -tcsh (tcsh)
% kill 544
# Terminated
taylor   console  Feb  6 08:02
taylor   ttyp1    Feb  6 08:30
taylor   ttyp2    Feb  6 08:32

[1]    Done                   ( sleep 60; who )
```

We decided that 60 seconds was too long to wait for the output of who. The ps listing showed that sleep had the process ID number 544, so we use this PID to kill the sleep process. You should see a message like "terminated" or "killed"; if you don't, use another ps command to be sure the process has been killed.

The who program is executed immediately, as it is no longer waiting on sleep; it lists the users logged into the system.

Problem checklist

The process didn't die when I told it to.

Some processes can be hard to kill. If a normal kill of these processes is not working, enter kill -9 *PID*. This is a sure kill and can destroy almost anything, including the shell that is interpreting it.

In addition, if you've run an interpreted program (such as a shell script), you may not be able to kill all dependent processes by killing the interpreter process that got it all started; you may need to kill them individually. However, killing a process that is feeding data into a pipe generally kills any processes receiving that data.

CHAPTER 10

Where to Go from Here

Now that you're almost to the end of this guide, let's look at some ways to continue learning about Unix. Documentation is an obvious choice, but it isn't always in obvious places. You can save time by taking advantage of other shell features—aliases, functions, and scripts—that let you shorten a repetitive job and "let the computer do the dirty work."

We'll close by seeing how you can use Unix commands on non-Unix systems.

Documentation

You might want to know the options to the programs we've introduced and get more information about them and the many other Unix programs. You're now ready to consult your system's documentation and other resources.

The man Command

Different versions of Unix have adapted Unix documentation in different ways. Almost all Unix systems have documentation derived from a manual originally called the *Unix Programmer's Manual*. The manual has numbered sections; each section is a collection of manual pages, often called manpages; each program has its own manpage. Section 1 has manpages for general Unix programs such as who and ls.

Mac OS X has individual manual pages stored on the computer; users can read them online. If your system has online manpages, and you want to know the correct syntax for entering a command or the particular features of a program, enter the command man and the name of the command. The syntax is:

```
man command
```

For example, if you want to find information about the program mail, which allows you to send messages to other users, enter:

```
% man mail
.
.
.
%
```

The output of man is filtered through a pager in Mac OS X like **less** automatically. If it isn't, just pipe the output of man to less (or more or pg).

After you enter the command, the screen fills with text. Press the spacebar or Return to read more, and q to quit.

Mac OS X also includes a command called apropos or man -k to help you locate a command if you have an idea of what it does but are not sure of its correct name. Enter apropos followed by a descriptive word; you'll get a list of commands that might help. To get this working, however, you need to first build the apropos database. This can be done with the following command (you'll need sudo enabled for this to work):

```
% sudo /usr/libexec/makewhatis
Password:
%
```

Now you can use apropos to find all commands related to PostScript, for example, with:

```
% man -k postscript
enscript(1)            - convert text files to PostScript
grops(1)               - PostScript driver for groff
pfbtops(1)             - translate a PostScript font in .pfb format to
ASCII
psbb(1)                - extract bounding box from PostScript document
```

Problem checklist

man says there is no manual entry for the command.

Some commands—cd and jobs, for example—aren't separate Unix programs; they're part of the shell. On some Unix systems, you'll find documentation for those commands in the manual page for the shell. (To find the shell's name, see the section "The Unix Shell" in Chapter 1.)

If the program isn't a standard part of your Unix system—that is, your system staff added the program to your system—there may not be a manual page, or you may have to configure the man program to find the local manpage files. The third possibility for this is that you don't have all the manpage directories in your MANPATH variable. If so, add the following to your *.cshrc*, then quit and restart Terminal.

```
setenv MANPATH "/usr/share/man:/usr/local/share/man:/usr/X11R6/man:/sw/
share/man"
```

Documentation via the Internet

The Internet changes so quickly that any list of online Unix documentation we'd give you would soon be out of date. Still, the Internet is a great place to find out about Unix systems. Remember that there are many different versions of Unix, so some documentation you find may not be completely right for you. Also, some information you'll find may be far too technical for your needs (many computer professionals use and discuss Unix). But don't be discouraged! Once you've found a site with the general kind of information you need, you can probably come back later for more.

The premier place to start your exploration of online documentation for Mac OS X Unix is the Apple web site. But don't start on their home page. Start either on their Mac OS X page (*http://www.apple.com/macosx/*) or their Darwin project home page (*http://www.opensource.apple.com/*). Another excellent place to get information about software downloads and add-ons to your Unix world is the Fink project (*http://fink.sourceforge.net/*).

Many Unix command names are plain English words, which can make searching hard. If you're looking for collections of Unix information, try searching for the Unix program named grep. As this book went to press, one especially Unix-friendly search engine was Google, at *http://www.google.com*.

Here are some other places to try:

Magazines
Both print and online magazines have Unix tutorials and links to more information. Many are written for beginners.

Publishers
Those such as O'Reilly & Associates, Inc. (*http://www.oreilly.com*), have areas of their web sites that feature Unix and have articles written by their books' authors. They may also have books online (such as the O'Reilly Safari service) available for a small monthly fee—which is a good way to learn a lot quickly without needing to buy a paper copy of a huge book, most of which you might not need.

Universities
Many schools use Unix-like systems and will have online documentation. You'll probably have better luck at the Computer Services division (which services the whole campus) than at the Computer Science department (which may be more technical).

OS X–related web sites
Many are worthy of note, though they're run by third parties and may change by the time you read this. Mac OS X Apps (*http://www. macosxapps.com*) offers a wide variety of Aqua applications,

Information on Darwin can be found at Darwinfo (*http://www.darwinfo.org*), and Mac OS X Hints (*http://www.macosxhints.com*) all offer valuable information and hints. One more site well worth a bookmark is O'Reilly's MacDevCenter (*http://www.oreilly.com/mac/*).

Books

Bookstores, both traditional and online, are full of computer books. The books are written for a wide variety of needs and backgrounds. Unfortunately, many books are rushed to press, written by authors with minimal Unix experience, full of errors. Before you buy a book, read through parts of it. Does the style (brief or lots of detail, chatty and friendly or organized as a reference) fit your needs? Search the Internet for reviews; online bookstores may have readers' comments on file.

Shell Aliases and Functions

If you type command names that are hard for you to remember, or command lines that seem too long, you'll want to learn about *shell aliases* and *shell functions*. These shell features let you abbreviate commands, command lines, and long series of commands. In most cases, you can replace them with a single word or a word and a few arguments. For example, one of the long pipelines (see the section "Pipes and Filters" in Chapter 6) could be replaced by an alias or function named (for instance, aug). When you type aug at a shell prompt, the shell would list files modified in August, sorted by size.

Making an alias or function is almost as simple as typing in the command line or lines that you want to run. References in the section "Documentation" earlier in this chapter, have more information. Shell aliases and functions are actually a simple case of shell programming.

Programming

We mention earlier that the shell is the system's command interpreter. It reads each command line you enter at your terminal and performs the operation that you call for. Your shell is chosen when your account is set up.

The shell is just an ordinary program that can be called by a Unix command. However, it contains some features (such as variables, control structures, and so on) that make it similar to a programming language. You can save a series of shell commands in a file, called a *shell script*, to accomplish specialized functions.

Programming the shell should be attempted only when you are reasonably confident in your ability to use Unix commands. Unix is quite a powerful tool and its capabilities become more apparent when you try your hand at shell programming.

Take time to learn the basics. Then, when you're faced with a new task, take time to browse through references to find programs or options that will help you get the job done more easily. Once you've done that, learn how to build shell scripts so that you never have to type a complicated command sequence more than once.

You might also want to learn Perl. Like the shell, Perl interprets script files full of commands. But Perl has a steeper learning curve than the shell. Also, because you've already learned a fair amount about the shell and Unix commands by reading this book, you're almost ready to start writing shell scripts now; on the other hand, Perl will take longer to learn. But if you have sophisticated needs, learning Perl is another way to use even more of the power of your Unix system.

Configuring Sendmail

In the voodoo land of Unix, nothing is more weird and confusing than the low-level mechanism used for sending mail. Mac OS X Unix includes sendmail, a powerful but incredibly complex application that manages communication between command-line mail user agents (such as Pine) and the Internet itself.

Unfortunately, Mac OS X has default settings that make it impossible for you to send mail directly from the command line. If you do, you'll probably see an error similar to:

```
% mail -s practice taylor@intuitive.com < /dev/null
sendmail: cannot open /etc/mail/local-host-names: Group writable directory
%
```

The fix is straightforward, and involves a single tweak!

All you need to do is change the permission of the root directory with chmod (and enter your password when prompted):

```
% sudo chmod 755 /
password:
%
```

and sendmail should work fine. If you want to also configure your system to receive mail (that is, run as a mail server), you'll need to make one additional change.

To configure your server for receiving email, you need to change the configuration of your system so that it knows you want to run a mail server. Make the following two changes to the file */etc/hostconfig*:

```
Change MAILSERVER=-NO- to MAILSERVER=-YES-
Change HOSTNAME=-AUTOMATIC- to HOSTNAME=host.your.domain
```

Here's how my *letc/hostconfig* looks after these modifications (we've high-lighted the two changed lines in bold to have them stand out a bit more):

```
# cat /etc/hostconfig
##
# /etc/hostconfig
##
# This file is maintained by the system control panels
##

# Network configuration
HOSTNAME=dsl-138.dsldesigns.net
ROUTER=-AUTOMATIC-

# Services
AFPSERVER=-NO-
APPLETALK=en0
AUTHSERVER=-NO-
AUTOMOUNT=-YES-
CONFIGSERVER=-NO-
IPFORWARDING=-NO-
MAILSERVER=-YES-
MANAGEMENTSERVER=-NO-
NETINFOSERVER=-AUTOMATIC-
RPCSERVER=-AUTOMATIC-
NETBOOTSERVER=-NO-
NISDOMAIN=-NO-
TIMESYNC=-YES-
QTSSERVER=-NO-
SSHSERVER=-NO-
WEBSERVER=-NO-
APPLETALK_HOSTNAME="Big G4 Computer"
```

To edit this file, use the command `sudo vi /etc/hostconfig` so that you can write the revised version back to your disk without permission problems cropping up.

That should do it. Reboot your system and you should be able to send and receive email from the Terminal.

Glossary

alphanumeric

Characters: letters (*alpha*) and numbers (*numeric*), including punctuation characters (such as _ and ?).

AppleTalk

A suite of transport protocols first introduced in Mac OS 7 and included in all systems since that release. One advantage of AppleTalk is that it's very easy to add and modify devices on an AppleTalk network.

Aqua

The graphical appearance and workspace of Mac OS X. In the world of the X Window System, Aqua would be called a window manager.

BSD

The Berkeley Software Distribution version of Unix, BSD was the academic Unix, compared to System V, from AT&T Bell Telephone Labs, which had more of a commercial bent.

click

Depress and quickly release a mouse button; double- and triple-click imply depressing and releasing a mouse button two or three times, respectively, within a short period. See also *point*.

clipboard

A temporary storage area for Mac OS X programs, used for transferring text ("copying" and "pasting" text) between programs.

command

An instruction that you can give to a program running on the Unix system. For instance, you can type a program's name and arguments on a command line, at a shell prompt; this command asks the shell to run that program. (The shell is a program itself; see *shell*.) Once a program starts running, it may accept commands of its own. For example, a text editor has commands for deleting and adding text to the file it's editing.

The terms *command* and *program* are used almost interchangeably, probably because the program name is typed first on a command line (at a shell prompt). Shells have some *built-in* commands that don't start a separate program running; one of these is cd, which changes the shell's working directory.

cracker

A malicious person who tries to break into computer systems (usually via a network), disrupt computers and networks, steal secrets (such as passwords and credit card numbers), and exhibit other antisocial behavior.

Popular media often call these people *hackers*. But, to most computer people, a hacker is someone who enjoys computing and programming, and may be an expert at some area of it. (For instance, a *Perl hacker* is someone who's good at programming in the Perl language.)

Darwin

A version of BSD Unix that serves as the underpinnings of Mac OS X (with the addition of Aqua).

Desktop

The part of a display that's "behind" (not enclosed within) the windows, icons, and other items on the display.

directory

A list of files and/or other directories. A directory is actually a special kind of file that has names and locations of other files and directories. See also *working directory*.

drag

As in *drag an object*, i.e., a window or an icon, means to point to the object and then depress and hold down (usually) the mouse button while moving the pointer to a new location, where the mouse button is released.

Mac OS X supports "drag and drop," which means dragging one object and dropping it over another object. For example, to print a file, you could drag the file's icon and drop it onto a printer icon.

Finder

A graphical filesystem browser for your Macintosh. Prior to Mac OS X, the only way you could interact with your system was through the Finder, but now you can also opt to use the Terminal.

Free Software Foundation (FSF)

An organization formed in 1985 that works for the rights of computer users to study, copy, modify, and redistribute computer programs. The

FSF also distributes free software. See *http://www.fsf.org/*; see also *GNU*.

GNU

A project, started in 1984, to develop a completely free Unix-like operating system: the GNU system. GNU stands for "GNU's Not Unix;" it is pronounced "guh-NEW." See also *Free Software Foundation*.

mouse pointer

The graphic symbol that appears on the output display and moves under the control of the mouse, trackball, or keyboard input to the window system.

multitasking

An operating system that can run more than one program at a time is said to be a *multitasking OS*. The programs don't actually all run simultaneously; the OS can divide the computer's time between the different programs very rapidly, so that they all *appear* to run at the same time. The system can still be overloaded and run slowly, if too many programs are trying to run at once.

Unix has always been multitasking, and Macintosh systems have been multitasking for many years too.

pathname

The location of a file or directory in a Unix filesystem: a series of names separated by slash (/) characters. Pathnames can be *absolute* (starting with a slash character, which means they begin at the filesystem's root directory) or *relative* (not starting with a slash, which means the pathname starts from the current working directory). See also the section "The Unix Filesystem" in Chapter 2.

point

As in "point a mouse," means to position the mouse pointer at a specified place or location within a window or other part of a window system display. See also *click, drag*.

program

A set of instructions to the computer, written by a programmer, and stored in a file. The program is executed when you type its name as the first word on a command line, at a shell prompt (or when you choose the program from a menu or icon in a window system). Unix runs a program as a *process*, which you can suspend or terminate using job control, an interrupt key, or the kill command.

root (user and directory)

Unix systems have an account named *root*, also called the "superuser," that has no protections or restrictions. System administrators and staff use this account to make changes to the system's configuration and operation.

A Unix filesystem is like an upside-down tree with a branching structure of directories inside directories. The first directory, where the filesystem starts, is called the *root directory*. Figure 2-1 is a filesystem diagram showing the root directory and a small part of a filesystem.

screen

The area of a terminal (usually glass or plastic) that shows computer output. See also *terminal*.

session

When two programs, or two users running programs, communicate across a network, they typically start the communication by doing a certain thing—for instance, by logging in. The communication continues until it's completed (or, possibly, aborted before it completes)—for instance, by logging out. The entire process, from start to completion, is called a *session*.

shell

A program that runs other programs. There are several different kinds of shells, each with its own command-line syntax; some of the most common are *bash*, *tcsh*, and *ksh*. All shells do the same basic job: reading commands that you type interactively at a shell prompt or reading commands noninteractively from a program file called a *shell script*.

When you start using Terminal, a shell program begins to run and prints a shell prompt. When you terminate that shell (by typing exit or Control-D at a prompt), you're logged out from that Terminal.

syntax

The rules for, or the format of, the characters you use to make a command or other computer input. For example, the syntax of a Unix command line is explained in the section "Syntax of Unix Command Lines" of Chapter 1.

window

An area of an output display often smaller in size than the maximum size of the display screen.

If a window manager program is running, a window will usually have a well-defined border, a title, and other characteristics. The Aqua window manager lets you move and resize a window as well.

working directory

When you give Unix a *relative* pathname to a file or subdirectory, the working directory is the starting point—the directory where that relative pathname starts. For example, if your working directory is */Users/joe/food* and you type the command less recipes/fish, Unix opens the file */Users/joe/food/recipes/fish*. (Your working directory is still */Users/joe/food*.)

If you type the command from any working directory, you get a listing of the files in your parent directory. That command uses the relative pathname to the parent directory (..). So if your working directory is /Users/joe/food, that command would list the parent directory /Users/joe. Or, if your working directory is /Users/joe, that same command would list the parent directory /Users.

Each process running on a Unix system has its own working directory, which the program can change at any time. For instance, you can give the shell the command cd to change its working directory.

Index

We'd like to hear your suggestions for improving our indexes. Send email to *index@oreilly.com*.

index (message) screens for
newsgroups, 106
input redirection operator (<), 72
input/output redirection (see I/O)
Internet, 81–90
remote logins, 81–84
transferring files, 84–90
Unix-based tools, 91–113
electronic mail, 93–103
Lynx, 91–93
Internet Relay Chat (IRC), 108–113
interpreted programs, 117
interrupt characters, 6, 11
I/O (input/output) redirection, 72
creating files, 36–41
IRC (Internet Relay Chat), 108–113

J

j command (vi), 41
⌘-J (Jump to Selection), 2
job control, 7, 114, 115
stopped jobs, 7
suspending jobs, 11
jobs command, 118
Joy, Bill, 37

K

k command (vi), 41
kill command, 11, 118
Korn shell (ksh), 2
ksh (Korn) shell, 2

L

l command (vi), 41
-l option (ls), 9, 78
lcd (ftp command), 87
LESS environment variable, 25
less program, 56, 79
using, 24
wildcards and, 35
less-than symbol (<), 72
links
in long formats, 22
in text-based browsers, 93
Linux, viii
locate program, 47
log files (printing), creating, 68
logging out, 6

logins (remote), 81–84
logout command, 6
long format of files, using -l option, 21
lpq program, 65
LPR printer, configuring, 67–71
lpr program, 65
lprm program, 67
ls program, 9, 20–29
chmod, setting permissions with, 27
rm command and, 48
Lynx web browser, 91–93

M

Mac OS X: The Missing Manual, x
Mac-format files, copying, 45
Mach microkernel, viii
mail (electronic), 93–103
mail program, 9, 72, 94
man program, 120
MANPATH variable, 121
message headers (Pine), 98
message index screens for
newsgroups, 106
mget (ftp command), 87
microkernel (Mach), viii
Microsoft Windows
accessing with Unix, 49
mkdir program, 42
modification date, 22
more program, 24
mput (ftp command), 87
multitasking, 114–119
multi-user operating system, vii
mv program, 46
MvMac program, 46

N

:n command (less), 25
-n grep option, 78
⌘-N, opening windows, 2
-n option command, 8
name in long formats, 22
ncftp program, 86, 88
Net News, 103
NetInfo database, 69
networked filesystems, 15
networks, copying files across, 84–90
news articles (newsgroups), 105
newsgroups, 103

$SHELL command, getting shell
    name, 3
Shell preferences, 51
shell programs, for configuring
    environment, 55
shells, 2
    aliases, 123
    environment, customizing, 55–60
    programming shell scripts, 123
    prompt, 3
    sending mail from, 94
Silverman, Richard, 84
sizes (bytes) in long formats, 22
slash (/)
    absolute pathnames and, 16
    finding patterns (vi), 39
    IRC, using, 110
    ls command and, 23
    root directories and, 14
    wildcards and, 35
sockets, 20
sort command, 78
    -o option, 8
sort program, 116
spool directories, creating, 68
ssh (secure shell) program, 82
SSH: The Secure Shell, 84
standard input/output, 72
Startup Preferences, 50
STAT (Run Time State), 116
subdirectories, 14
superusers, logging in as, 3
suspend characters, 115
suspending jobs, 11
symbolic links, 20
syntax of command lines, 7

T

T (take address) Pine command, 100
Tab key, completing file and directory
    names, 32
talk program, 107
tcsh shell, 2
telnet program, 82
Terminal name (TT), 116
terminal windows, 1
    customizing sessions, 50–60
        launching, 50–55
    frozen, 11

multitasking in, 114
text
    appending to files, 76
    changing preferences, 52
    inserting into files, 73
    Lynx web browser, 91–93
    searching files for, 77
    sorting lines of, 78
text editors, 36
time, 4
TIME (Run time), 117
tmp directory, 14
total blocks in long formats (ls), 22
touch program, 19
tr command, translating carriage
    return, 37
trees (directories), 14, 19
troubleshooting
    command line, 5
    logging out, 7
    overwriting files by mistake, 74
TT (Terminal name), 116
tty program, 116
type in long formats (ls), 22

U

⌘-U, erasing lines of input, 6
u (user) permission, 27
UC Berkeley, viii
Unix, viii
    accessing other platforms, 49
    Aqua carriage returns and, 37
    commands, xi
    customizing sessions, 50–60
    documentation on, 120
    environment, 1–7
    Internet tools for, 91–113
    using, 13–32
    versions of, ix
Unix Power Tools, 56, 60
Unix Programmer's Manual, 120
up-arrow key, recalling previous
    commands, 5
U.S. Department of Defense Advanced
    Research Projects Agency, viii
Usenet news, 103
user (u) permission, 27
usernames, 1
    mailing to, 94

users
  access modes for, 22
  who program for, 74
users directory, 14, 17
Using csh and tcsh, 55, 60
usr directory, 14

V

v command (less), 25
vertical bar (|) for I/O redirection, 73, 76
vi text editor, 25, 36–41
vim text editor, 41

W

:w command (vi), 41
w program, 10
W (Whereis) Pine command, 101
w (write) permission, 22, 27
web browsers
  FTP (File Transfer Protocol) and, 89
  Lynx, 91, 91–93
where is (vi command), 39
Whereis (W) Pine command, 101

who am i program, 4
who program, 4, 74
  options and, 8
wildcards, 28, 34
  copying files, 43
  less program and, 35
  removing files and, 48
window preferences, 52
/word command (less), 25
?word command (less), 25
word processors, 36
working directories, 14, 18
:wq command (vi), 41
write (w) permission, 22, 27

X

x (execute) permission, 22, 27
X (Set/Unset) command, 102

Z

Z Shell (zsh), 2
zsh (Z) shell, 2
ZZ command (vi), 41

About the Author

Dave Taylor is a popular writer, teacher, and speaker focused on business and technology issues. He is the founder of The Internet Mall and *iTrack.com* and has been involved with Unix and the Internet since 1980, having created the popular Elm mail system. He's also been a Mac fan since their original release, when he started out with a dirty beige Mac Plus. Previous positions include being a research scientist at HP Laboratories and senior reviews editor of *SunWorld* magazine. He has contributed software to the official 4.4 release of Berkeley Unix (BSD), and his programs are found in all versions of Linux and other popular Unix variants.

Jerry Peek is a longtime user of the Unix operating system. He has acted as a Unix consultant, courseware developer, and instructor. Coupling his knowledge of Unix with his technical writing skills makes Jerry the perfect author to provide the beginning Unix user with a solid introduction to the operating system.

Colophon

Our look is the result of reader comments, our own experimentation, and feedback from distribution channels. Distinctive covers complement our distinctive approach to technical topics, breathing personality and life into potentially dry subjects.

The animal on the cover of *Learning Unix for Mac OS X* is an Alaskan malamute. The Alaskan malamute is one of the oldest Arctic sled dogs. These powerful dogs have muscular bodies, structured for strength and endurance. They have broad heads with bulky muzzles and triangular ears, which stand erect to signify alertness. Their thick coats are coarse and dark on the outside, with soft, wooly undercoats.

Alaskan malamutes make excellent companions, as they are affectionate, friendly, and loyal. They can be playful, but tend to become more reserved as they mature. They are very intelligent, with eyes that reveal their curiosity and interest.

Linley Dolby was the production editor and copyeditor for *Learning Unix for Mac OS X*. Emily Quill, Darren Kelly, and Claire Cloutier provided quality control. Joe Wizda wrote the index.

Emma Colby designed the cover of this book, based on a series design by Edie Freedman. The cover image is an illustration from the *Illustrated Natural History: Mammalia*. Emma Colby produced the cover layout with QuarkXPress 4.1 using Adobe's ITC Garamond font.

David Futato designed the interior layout. This book was converted to FrameMaker 5.5.6 with a format conversion tool created by Erik Ray, Jason McIntosh, Neil Walls, and Mike Sierra that uses Perl and XML technologies. The text font is Linotype Birka; the heading font is Adobe Myriad Condensed; and the code font is LucasFont's TheSans Mono Condensed. The illustrations that appear in the book were produced by Robert Romano and Jessamyn Read using Macromedia FreeHand 9 and Adobe Photoshop 6. The tip and warning icons were drawn by Christopher Bing. This colophon was written by Linley Dolby.

Other Titles Available from O'Reilly

Macintosh Power Users

Mac OS X: The Missing Manual

By David Pogue
1st Edition December 2001
596 pages, ISBN 0-596-00082-0

The fact that the Mac OS X comes without a printed manual is a real problem, since Mac OS X is so different from the operating system that came before it. Now David Pogue, the number one best-selling Macintosh author, fills the gap with the definitive guide to Mac OS X. His trademark wit and clarity brings to this new software world the same sense of reassurance, surprise, and delight that made bestsellers of his *Mac OS 9: The Missing Manual* and *iMovie 2: The Missing Manual*.

Mac OS X Pocket Reference

By Chuck Toporek
1st Edition May 2002
128 pages, ISBN 0-596-00346-3

This is your guide to unleashing the power of Mac OS X. A perfect pocket-sized book that's easy to take anywhere, the *Mac OS X Pocket Reference* shows you how to use tools such as the Finder and the Dock, and includes an overview of the System Preferences, the Terminal application, and the Developer Tools. Also contained in this handy book are quick references for creating special characters, a listing of basic keyboard commands, and many tips and tricks for working with Mac OS X.

REALbasic: The Definitive Guide, 2nd Edition

By Matt Neuburg
2nd Edition September 2001
752 pages, ISBN 0-596-00177-0

Design astonishingly fast, full-fledged Mac applications with REALbasic! Even if you're a beginning programmer, this book will teach you the essential concepts for programming every aspect of REALbasic. It's a vital reference for the expanding legion of developers who are discovering the power and flexibility of REALbasic. Now covers REALbasic 3, so you can generate your project for Mac OS 8/9, Mac OS X, and Windows.

AppleScript in a Nutshell

By Bruce W. Perry
1st Edition June 2001
528 pages, ISBN 1-56592-841-5

AppleScript in a Nutshell is the first complete reference to AppleScript, the popular programming language that gives both power users and sophisticated enterprise customers the important ability to automate repetitive tasks and customize applications. *AppleScript in a Nutshell* is a high-end handbook at a low-end price—an essential desktop reference that puts the full power of this user-friendly programming language into every AppleScript user's hands.

Office X for Macintosh: The Missing Manual

By Nan Barber, Tonya Engst & David Reynolds
1st Edition July 2002
728 pages, ISBN 0-596-00332-3

This book applies the urbane and readable Missing Manuals touch to a winning topic: Microsoft Office X for Apple's stunning new operating system, Mac OS X. In typical Missing Manual style, targeted sidebars ensure that the book's three sections impart business-level details on Word, Excel, and the Palm-syncable Entourage, without leaving beginners behind. Indispensable reference for a growing user base.

Macintosh Developers

Learning Cocoa with Objective-C

By James Duncan Davidson &
Apple Computer, Inc.
2nd Edition September 2002 (est.)
384 pages (est.), ISBN 0-596-00301-3

Based on the Jaguar release of
Mac OS X 10.2, this new edition
of *Learning Cocoa* covers the latest updates to the Cocoa frameworks, including
examples that use the Address Book and Universal
Access APIs. Also included with this edition is a
handy quick reference card, charting Cocoa's Foundation and AppKit frameworks, along with an
Appendix that includes a listing of resources essential
to any Cocoa developer—beginning or advanced.

Learning Carbon

By Apple Computer, Inc.
1st Edition May 2001
368 pages, ISBN 0-596-00161-4

Get up to speed quickly on creating Mac OS X applications with
Carbon. You'll learn the funda-
mentals and key concepts of Carbon programming as you design and build a
complete application under the book's guidance.
Written by insiders at Apple Computer, *Learning
Carbon* provides information you can't get anywhere else, giving you a head start in the Mac OS X
application development market.

Learning Unix for the Mac OS X

By Dave Taylor & Jerry Peek
1st Edition May 2002
160 pages, ISBN 0-596-00342-0

This concise introduction offers
just what readers need to know
for getting started with Unix
functions on Mac OS X. Mac
users have long been comfortable
with the easy-to-use elegance of the Mac GUI, and
are loathe to change. With Mac OS X, they can continue using their preferred platform and explore the
powerful capabilities of Unix at the same time.
Learning Unix for the Mac OS X tells readers how
to use the Terminal application, become functional
with the command interface, explore many Unix
applications, and—most important—how to take
advantage of the strengths of both interfaces.

Building Cocoa Applications: A Step-by-Step Guide

By Simson Garfinkel &
Mike Mahoney
1st Edition May 2002
648 pages, ISBN 0-596-00235-1

Building Cocoa Applications is a
step-by-step guide to developing
applications for Apple's Mac OS X. It describes, in
an engaging tutorial fashion, how to build substantial, object-oriented applications using Cocoa. The
primary audience for this book is C programmers
who want to learn quickly how to use Cocoa to
build significant Mac OS X applications. The book
takes the reader from basic Cocoa functions
through the most advanced and powerful facilities.

How to stay in touch with O'Reilly

1. Visit our award-winning web site

http://www.oreilly.com/

★ "Top 100 Sites on the Web"—PC Magazine
★ CIO Magazine's Web Business 50 Awards

Our web site contains a library of comprehensive product information (including book excerpts and tables of contents), downloadable software, background articles, interviews with technology leaders, links to relevant sites, book cover art, and more. File us in your bookmarks or favorites!

2. Join our email mailing lists

Sign up to get email announcements of new books and conferences, special offers, and O'Reilly Network technology newsletters at:

http://www.elists.oreilly.com

It's easy to customize your free elists subscription so you'll get exactly the O'Reilly news you want.

3. Get examples from our books

To find example files for a book, go to:

http://www.oreilly.com/catalog

select the book, and follow the "Examples" link.

4. Work with us

Check out our web site for current employment opportunites:

http://jobs.oreilly.com/

5. Register your book

Register your book at:

http://register.oreilly.com

6. Contact us

O'Reilly & Associates, Inc.
1005 Gravenstein Hwy North
Sebastopol, CA 95472 USA
TEL: 707-827-7000 or 800-998-9938
(6am to 5pm PST)
FAX: 707-829-0104

order@oreilly.com
For answers to problems regarding your order or our products. To place a book order online visit:

http://www.oreilly.com/order_new/

catalog@oreilly.com
To request a copy of our latest catalog.

booktech@oreilly.com
For book content technical questions or corrections.

corporate@oreilly.com
For educational, library, and corporate sales.

proposals@oreilly.com
To submit new book proposals to our editors and product managers.

international@oreilly.com
For information about our international distributors or translation queries. For a list of our distributors outside of North America check out:

http://international.oreilly.com/distributors.html

O'REILLY®

To order: *800-998-9938* • *order@oreilly.com* • *www.oreilly.com*
Online editions of most O'Reilly titles are available by subscription at *safari.oreilly.com*
Also available at most retail and online bookstores.